Office and Career Management for the Eyecare Paraprofessional

Office and Career Management for the Eyecare Paraprofessional

Bill Borover
Gracie Enterprises
Chula Vista, California

Tammy Langley, COT
Eyesight Associates
Warner Robins, Georgia

 The Basic Bookshelf for Eyecare Professionals

Series Editors: Janice K. Ledford • Ken Daniels • Robert Campbell

SLACK Incorporated, 6900 Grove Road, Thorofare, NJ 08086-9447

Publisher: John H. Bond
Editorial Director: Amy E. Drummond
Creative Director: Linda Baker
Assistant Editor: Miriam Priest

The following portions of the manuscript were written and contributed by Janice K. Ledford, COMT, of EyeWrite Productions: Accounts Payable in Chapter 4; sidebars "What the Patient Needs to Know" in Chapters 1 and 4; Talking About Salary, Traditional Benefits, Other Benefits, and portions of Interview Legalities in Chapter 6; Certification in Chapter 7; Burnout in Chapter 8; and in the Appendix, the Sample Résumé.

Borover, William A.
    Office and career management for the eye care paraprofessional/
    William A. "Bill" Borover, Tammy Langley.
        p. cm. — (The basic bookshelf for eyecare professionals;2)
    Includes bibliographical references and index.
    ISBN 1-55642-331-4
    1. Ophthalmic assistants. I. Langley, Tammy
II. Title. III. Series.
    [DNLM: 1. Practice Management, Medical. 2. Allied Health
Personnel. 3. Vocational Guidance. W 80 B7362o 1997]
RE72.5.B67 1997
617.7'0068—dc21
DNLM/DLC
for Library of Congress   96-51005

Printed in the United States of America
Published by: SLACK Incorporated
                6900 Grove Road
                Thorofare, NJ 08086-9447 USA
                Telephone: 609-848-1000
                Fax: 609-853-5991

Contact SLACK Incorporated for more information about other books in this field or about the availability of our books from distributors outside the United States.

Last digit is print number: 10 9 8 7 6 5 4 3 2 1

Dedication

Although I have authored seven books I remain awed at the understanding and support of my wife Gracie. Her encouragement, insight, inspiration, support, prompting, and proofreading has once again made the impossible perfectly possible.

BB

If words could be used to convey the depth of my dedication and love for the three most important aspects of my life, those words would be printed here. Since there are no such words, and you can't hear the music in my heart, I must simply say that to God, my husband Jim, and my children Josh and Chris, I dedicate this book . . . as a token of gratitude for the blessing of sharing your lives.

TL

Contents

Section I. Office Procedures

Section II. Career Management

Appendix: Forms 95

Acknowledgments

A special thank you to Viola Nelson and her magic word processing wizardry. Even though she has typed innumerable documents, I am still dumbfounded by her accuracy, timeliness, and flawless sense of syntax.

BB

Special thanks goes out to Susan Dumont, Janet Morse, and Marvin Bittinger, MD, for graciously providing research materials. To Meg McClaine, director of the Rainbow House, thanks for your expert assistance with the abuse material, and Johnny Thomas who faithfully handles our account with the local newspaper. I also wish to thank my patients, who have taught me much.

TL

About The Authors

Bill Borover, speaker, lecturer, and author, was born in Cleveland, Ohio in 1939. Before entering the ophthalmic field, he spent a number of years as a professional magician. Then Bill earned a bachelor's in education and became an Educational Area Specialist for the Cuyahoga Community College Ophthalmic Technology Program. He implemented and coordinated Ohio's first ophthalmic assisting school, and became the program's leader and head instructor. Moving to Southern California in 1978, Bill became Executive Director of The Eye Physician's Medical/Surgical Center in Chula Vista, CA. In July of 1986, Bill began consulting full time for the ophthalmic professions. He has over 30 years of hands-on experience and has helped more than 2,000 eyecare practitioners. He lives in the San Diego area of Southern California with his life partner, Wendi Gracie.

Because of Bill's gratitude for having had the opportunity to learn from the eyecare professions, he has dedicated his life's work to the mission statement "Helping Eye Doctors With Their Vision."

Tammy Langley began her ophthalmic journey with the Air Force in 1980. "Landing" in Warner Robins, GA, Tammy is currently employed by Eyesight Associates, and has expanded her career to include medical marketing. She is also the Executive Producer of "Eyesight Insights," a 30-minute television program about eyecare. Believing that no one is self-made, she welcomes the opportunity to help others become successful in their quest to provide quality health care.

The Study Icons

The *Basic Bookshelf For Eyecare Professionals* is quality educational material designed for professionals in all branches of eyecare. Because so many of you want to expand your careers, we have made a special effort to include information needed for certification exams. When these study icons appear in the margin of a *Series* book, it is your cue that the material next to the icon is listed as a criteria item for a certification examination. Please use this key to identify the appropriate icon:

OptA	optometric assistant
OptT	optometric technician
OphA	ophthalmic assistant
OphT	ophthalmic technician
OphMT	ophthalmic medical technologist
LV	low vision subspecialty
Srg	ophthalmic surgical assisting subspecialty
CL	contact lens registry
Optn	opticianry
RA	retinal angiographer
OPRA	ophthalmic photographer and retinal angiographer

Section I

OFFICE PROCEDURES

Chapter 1

Records Management

- The contents of a chart are medical/legal documents and must be handled appropriately.

- Recall is an insurance policy to future business and is one of the most important result-producing activities of the office.

- Office forms are a convenient method of compiling information vital to the patient and the practice.

Chart Management

 The primary purpose for keeping medical records is to fully document the patient's visit and progress. It also represents security in case of an audit from a government or private peer review organization.

Medical records may be organized and filed in an alphabetic or numeric style, or both. The most ideal system is one in which patients' records and/or information may be obtained from the following:

1. Last name
2. First name
3. Address
4. Social security number

One of the best manual systems for labeling charts is through the use of a self-adhering tab that denotes letters of the patient's first and last name in a brightly colored, easy-to-see form. For example, the tab carries the initial letters BO, representing the first two letters in the last name of Borover. These letters are followed by WI, indicating the first two letters of the patient's first name, as in William. Adjacent to the last two letters are two numbers representing the year in which the patient was last seen. Thus, a tab indicating BOWI97 represents a chart for William Borover who was last seen in 1997.

Developing a standard operating procedure or protocol for patient records is the easiest way to ensure both maintenance and organization. One great advantage of color coding charts with brightly colored labels or tabs is that a misfiled chart is easy to spot. For example, if all of the BOs are blue, it is easy to see an odd-colored chart among them quickly.

The more information that can be acquired at a glance of the patient's medical record, the better the service that can be delivered to the patient. Using a distinctive color for the patient record holder or cover, or a brightly colored label on the front of the cover, can help the staff distinguish between certain types of patients (such as Medicare, Medicaid, health maintenance organization [HMO], very important person [VIP], etc.). The staff may use any modality as long as it is consistent. Additionally, a master list of these labels, abbreviations, or other personalized markings should be kept in a notebook, or prominently posted near the filing area. This way, any staff member can quickly identify the symbols.

Because all patient record charts require maintenance, it is important for a successful office to develop a maintenance program in which all charts that are frayed or in disrepair are set aside and a staff member can then repair them before refiling.

Because paper charts become thick and cumbersome with many patient visits, it is important to develop a system for purging them. Most eyecare practitioners keep a minimum number of charts in one place at one time. No greater than 4 to 5 years of charts should be in one cabinet at a time. Alternatives for chart storage include converting files to microfiche, storing files off-site, or scanning them into a computer file.

Even though elements of the patient record cover may be manipulated and altered through the use of color, symbols, labels, etc., it is important to remember that the contents of the chart itself are medical/legal documents and must be handled appropriately. Here are the guidelines for making a correction to patient records:

1. Never use correction fluid or erasures on the medical chart itself.
2. If a change needs to be made, then strike a line through the inaccuracy and write the correction clearly next to it.
3. Place your initials next to the correction.

Occasionally, a patient may leave the practice and need his or her medical records. Records release forms are legal documents authorizing the transfer of patient records to another physician or to the patient (Form 1, Appendix). It is important to remember that the medical charts and records belong to the patient as his or her sole property and may not be transferred without the owner's consent. It is wise to document the receipt and issuance of patient records in the patient's chart before photocopying, faxing, or otherwise transferring the record. The patient's record request should be signed by the patient, power of attorney, or legal guardian.

What the Patient Needs to Know

- The information in the medical record belongs to you, the patient.

- The physical chart belongs to the practice.

- The records may not be available immediately and it may take some time (several days) to process a transfer request.

- Instead of copying every single page, the eye care physician may elect to dictate a letter covering your care and progress as a summary.

- In almost every case your signature is required before records or any information can be released.

It is illegal to withhold a patient's record because he or she owes the practice money. It is legal, however, to include a copy of the patient's financial history with the medical records themselves. 
Other communication with regard to the patient's medical records is also considered a legal-ity. Giving anyone information from a patient's chart over the telephone or through a fax com-munication may breach patient confidentiality. The person requesting the information and his or her reason for the request should be carefully screened before any information is divulged. 

Recall

Few business activities produce more results than recall. It is, in a sense, an insurance policy to future business and should take its place as one of the most important activities the indepen-dent practitioner can organize and implement. 

Under the most ideal circumstances, a patient is reappointed for the next visit at the end of his or her initial visit, saving the cost and time of sending recall cards. In this instance, the patient merely needs to be reminded of the appointment time. Most offices accomplish this effectively by simply telephoning the patient several days in advance of the appointment. Because it is often challenging to pinpoint a specific date a year in advance, the most effective recall system is com-posed of three tiers, as follows:

Tier Number 1, Postcard

A postcard invites the patient to call and reappoint. The wording on this postcard should state the importance of the revisit, as well as an implied continuing relationship with the office or prac-tice. Because the art of scheduling can only be effective if the specific reason for visitation is known, this postcard can be encoded to provide the necessary information. For example: By printing a message such as "Thank You" along the bottom of the card, each letter of the words "Thank You" can represent a specific type of visit. Therefore, by simply circling this letter before mailing the card, a mechanism for communication has been established. When the patient calls to reappoint after receiving their card, the independent practitioner's staff can simply ask, "Do you have your postcard in front of you?" The answer is usually "Yes" because this is the easiest access to the practice's telephone number. The staff member then continues with, "On the bottom of the card, one of the letters is circled. Can you tell me which one it is?" The patient responds with the appropriate letter and the practice now knows that this recall is for a particular type of visit, as follows: T stands for contact lens follow-up; H stands for cataract; E stands for glaucoma; etc. Thus, reasons for return visits can be specifically identified and patients can be queried as to how they are feeling, and if they have additional complaints, etc. This mechanism also makes it unnecessary to pull a chart or record every time a patient calls.

Tier Number 2, Letter

The most effective recall systems send a formal letter to the patient or customer within 30 days of a nonresponse to the postcard. Whereas postcards can sometimes be overlooked or even lost, patients almost always open official-looking letters. Therefore, it is prudent to develop a professional looking official type of letter to the patient or customer. This letter should be created on quality paper and letterhead, and ideally should be produced on a laser-quality printer. The letters themselves can be word processed with macro preprepared paragraphs to make the process even easier. There are some existing resources that have programs for this type of activity. Because the recall letter can pinpoint the reason for the visit, it is unnecessary to use a coding program; however, assigning codes to the letter is also possible.

Tier Number 3, Personalized Phone Call

Within 10 days of a nonresponse to a letter, the practice should call the patient and inquire as to the status of the revisit. This is best accomplished with a sincere inquiry as to the patient's health or condition and can be expressed as the following script: "Hello Mr. Borover. This is Bill from Dr. Isee's office and Dr. Isee has asked me to call to find out if you are okay. He has indicated that he has sent you several notices to remind you of your revisit to the office and he has not heard anything from you. Are you okay?" This sincere type of approach usually can elicit the real reason the patient has not returned.

One of the key elements to a successful recall system is preparedness. If the office is prepared with accurate information about the patient's previous visitation, the inquiry remains professional and caring. Nonpreparation frequently results in an impression of commercialism. In a recent study of successful practices, (conducted by the author), recall played the greatest role in distinguishing mediocre practices from excellent practices. Although many independent practitioners feel you shouldn't have to ask for the sale, reality indicates otherwise.

One well-known consultant recently asked an independent practitioner, "Doctor, did you receive anything from Sak's Fifth Avenue in the mail today?" The surprised practitioner responded, "Well, no." Whereupon the consultant continued with, "Well, did you order anything from Sak's Fifth Avenue today?" Perhaps that was the reason that nothing came.

Office Forms

One of the most important forms any eyecare office can perfect is that of Initial Patient Registration (Form 2, Appendix). There are several methods of obtaining information on the initial patient information form. The first and most common method is to have the patient fill out forms when he or she arrives. It is wise to always book the patient sufficiently ahead of time to allow for completion of the paperwork before the appointed exam time. A second method uses the advantage of mailing a registration packet to the prospective patient, both welcoming him or her to the practice and inviting the patient to fill out the office forms ahead of time. The third method is to interview the patient by telephone prior to the exam and input the coordination of benefits and demographics in "real" time.

One very important portion of the patient registration form is the referring source field (Form 2, Appendix). It is imperative for good eye care practice management to have this field completed consistently. Referring source fields should designate the referring source by name and title. For example, referred by Bill Borover, PhD, DDS, DVM, OD, MD, DO, etc.

The second major office form is called the Interval Visit Registration form (Form 3, Appendix). This form is typically shorter and is used primarily to update the patient's demographics and coordination of benefits each time the patient presents. Even though patients frequently resent refilling out forms, it is important that their data is updated and, if necessary, changed. Patients frequently change insurance benefits and the best way to handle this is to let the patient know in a very caring way that the information is for his or her benefit.

When the patient feels that the information requested is for his or her doctor rather than the office, he or she is frequently more compliant. A sample script for this is as follows: "Before Dr. Borover sees you today, he has requested that you complete the follow-up or revisit form so that he may know of any changes in your information." Avoiding the use of the first person "I" helps patient compliance and attitude toward the office visit.

Besides patient registration, there are several special documents used by the contemporary eyecare office:

A Records Release Form (Form 1, Appendix) is a legal document signed by the patient, authorizing in writing the release of his or her records to either himself or herself, or a transfer of those records to another physician.

An Authorization for Payment (Form 4, Appendix) form authorizes the assigning of payments received from a third-party source to the doctor providing the service. This prevents third-party checks or payments from going directly to the patient, which can be confusing. Patients frequently think that there has been some sort of an error on the part of the insurance company and this money actually belongs to them. They fail to tell the office about the check while the practice is still awaiting the money. Meanwhile, the patient may have already spent the money and forgotten about it.

An Authorization for Responsibility (Form 5, Appendix) form documents who is responsible for the payment. Typically this is the patient, but it may be a power of attorney, a guardian, or another family member.

Waivers of Liability are used to inform the patient that a particular procedure or service may not be covered and, therefore, remains his or her financial responsibility (Form 6, Appendix).

Informed Consent documents are used to communicate the acceptance of a service or procedure (usually surgical). This informed consent includes, but is not limited to, the patient's acceptance of the risks, benefits, and procedural actions that are to be performed on them. Informed consents may be written or videotaped (Form 7, Appendix).

Computerization

As world communication becomes electronic, the eyecare practitioner should realize that a conversion from a paper system to a paperless one is a necessity rather than a desire. Whereas paper suffices for the documentation of certain graphic data such as visual fields and photography, all other data may be more easily stored and retrieved in an electronic form.

With the explosion of high technology radiating on the eyecare profession, today's management team is faced with a major challenge: how to best integrate 21st century technology into 20th century practices. Some of these challenges are staff acceptance, training and mastery, space and usage planning, scheduling and patient flow, and practice promotion.

The first step in managing high-tech magic is to understand that all magic imparts some fear. This is natural. However, the first step in overcoming fear is to understand how to best deal with it. It's not what one experiences that's important; it's what one does with the experience that's important. The most effective way to do something with fear is to run full force toward it.

An eyecare staff member recently commented, "I'm the kind of person who is terrified of technology. I would no more push buttons on that computer than I would look under the hood of my car." What this statement really expresses is fear. Fear of the unknown is the reason given most often for why integration of technology fails in eyecare practices. It is the most often cited reason for personnel leaving or being separated from their employment.

Question: How then, do eyecare practices overcome this?

Answer: By having a plan! Here's how it works:

1. Create a timetable for the arrival of new technology.
2. Create a training or orientation session on two levels. On the first level, include all staff. This could simply be an announcement such as "Borover Eye Center is proud to announce the acquisition of a new computer system. This system will help us save you time when you are in our office." The second level would be for those who will be using or directly interfacing with the high-tech device. You can help fearful users become more familiar with the device by creating a "faultless" practice session where orientation takes place in a leisurely manner and without negative repercussions. A representative from your computer company can probably assist in the staff training.
3. Plan for the space and/or all necessary auxiliaries: power, air vents, printer interface, etc.
4. Plan for scheduling, patient flow, and use.
5. Plan for aesthetic and ergonomic usage by ensuring that chairs are adjustable and computer screens are movable so there is the least amount of stress and strain on the eyes and back of the staff.
6. Plan a timetable for the practice to achieve mastery with the system/device.

In addition to handling finances (Chapter 4) and patient scheduling (Chapter 3) more easily, computerization will give you the ability to track the following key indicator ratios:

1. New patient ratio. This is formulated by dividing the number of new patients seen by the total number of patients seen, and is a measure of your success in generating new patients. A ratio that is too low prevents practice growth and a ratio that is too high indicates that patients may not be returning to you. The new patient average should range between 15% and 20%.
2. Expense ratio. This is calculated by dividing the total practice expenses by your collected revenues. The expense ratio of your practice should be somewhere between 50% and 60%.

3. Revenue per full-time equivalent ratio. This is calculated by taking all of your collected revenues and dividing by the number of full-time employees (equivalence). This is a measure of your efficiency. For example, if this ratio is too high it shows that you need to add staff.

Chapter 2

Marketing

- Taking advantage of co-op money can relieve the strain of an advertising budget.

- People who are representatives from other companies are liaisons between their employer and you, their client.

- Contracts are necessary to protect both the person buying advertising and the person selling advertising.

- Public speaking gives you a high profile in your community and adds to your credibility as a health care provider.

Promoting Services and Products

In today's highly competitive market, it is paramount that the general public be informed and aware of the services and products your practice makes available. Accomplishing this can be a challenge, but the results can be very rewarding for both your patients and your practice. Once the practice is established as a good resource for information, promoting new services will be perceived by your community as educating. The end result of your promotions will be an increase in your new patient base.

There are two basic ways you can promote a practice. Have a person from within your practice handle your program, or hire an advertising agency from the community. There are distinct advantages to each choice.

Having someone within the practice handle the advertising works well because he or she has firsthand knowledge of, and loyalty to your particular practice. Also, the physician or office manager/administrator is available to assist in making decisions in a timely manner and has easy access to the staff member. Financially, this will offset having to pay someone outside the practice.

Using an advertising agency can have its own set of advantages. They have a creative staff familiar with promoting, their relationships are already established within the advertising community, and they are very aware of how to place buys for all advertising media within your area. While they may have to be informed of the Food and Drug Administration's guidelines for medical marketing, they are already well-schooled in the promotion of retail, including optical products.

Marketing Budget

Once you have decided who is going to handle the promotion of the practice, it is time to hammer out a budget. A good guideline when starting is to allot 10% to 16% of your annual practice income. As you gain experience in the advertising arena and find what works best in your market, you can adjust the budget allotment to meet your needs. When you have devised a marketing plan, you can then designate a portion of the budget to each campaign and each medium you use.

If a particular product is involved in your advertising, there may be "co-op" money available to split expenses of the marketing fees. Co-op money is set aside by the company from which your practice purchases products. They will share marketing costs with you when your advertisement includes mention of their product. It is best to set this up at the beginning of the year with the company's representative (rep), even if you are not planning to run your marketing campaign for their product until later in the year. This way, the rep can set aside the money for your practice and not delegate it somewhere else. If the rep doesn't handle the co-op money decisions, he or she can provide a contact name for you. Here is an example of how this works: Let's say you want to run an ad campaign for tinted contact lenses manufactured by the Eye Look Great company. Your plan is to blitz the market in April with print, radio, and television ads. The first thing to do after establishing your marketing plan is to contact the rep from the Eye Look Great company. It is possible they already have the ad slicks for print, recorded radio spots, and television commercials completed. All you have to do is customize it with your doctor's name or practice logo, address, and telephone number. Then, as a bonus, Eye Look Great may co-op, meaning they will share the cost of the ads you run, be it print, television, or radio. What a great deal! The creation of the ads you will run has already been done, and you get help to pay for the promotion of your practice. This can really take some strain off your budget.

Marketing Representatives

Representatives are intermediaries between you and the company they represent. He or she is commonly known as a "rep." The relationship between you and your rep is crucial to your marketing success. A good rep can help guide you in developing the best marketing plan for your target market. As an example, if your practice is interested in marketing excimer laser surgery, the primary target market would be patients aged 21 to 49. Your rep will be able to supply you with information that shows when and how you are most likely to reach persons in that age range, especially when using television and radio. Once you have chosen the media through which you desire to advertise, it's time to make the call to the station or newspaper. For now, let's say we're calling television station "WEYE."

Once you've reached the receptionist at the station, ask to speak to the sales manager. He or she will be able to tell you if your practice already has a rep assigned to your account. Even if you have never advertised with them before, it is still possible that you have been targeted as a potential client. In either case, let the sales manager know you would like to schedule an appointment with your rep. It is customary for the rep to come to your office for the meeting. Before you actually meet your rep, make yourself some notes about your marketing ideas. One of the first things your rep will want to know is how he or she can help you achieve your advertising goal. Know your budget, target market (age, gender, income level, etc.), and if other advertising media will be involved such as radio or newsprint ads.

Once the meeting date has arrived and your rep reports to your office, greet him or her warmly. (Remember, you are the one who called the meeting; he or she is probably more anxious than you are!) Ask several questions about the station. You'll need to know what their ratings are (what share of the market they reach), and how those ratings are obtained. There are companies that can be hired to track how many people are being reached at any given time. They provide statistics to their clients on a quarterly basis. If the station you are dealing with doesn't subscribe to a ratings company, it is a good idea to move on to another station that does. It is imperative to know what share of the market you are reaching so that you can compare the costs with the amount of potential patients being reached. Demographics will tell you if "WEYE" has the strength to cover your entire market area. Find out if they will do the production for you, and if the cost for that production will be additional. If not, be specific in how much you will be investing in the production side of things. Be sure you are clear about this part of your contract! How much time will be required to create your commercial? What is the hourly rate for the camera crew? Does the rate include the equipment needed to achieve the desired effect? Who will write the script or ad copy? Is editing extra? What are the editing hourly rates?

When establishing your contract, remember to ask about "make good" spots, or bonus spots. "Make goods" are spots that will run if something goes wrong during the airing of your spots, such as the volume was wrong, there is a glitch in the tape, or part of the spot gets cut short, etc. If anything happens to affect your message as it goes out, it should be "made good" by another airing at no charge to your company. Bonus spots are spots that are aired on television or radio in addition to the schedule that you have bought. Often you can request bonus spots at the time you are negotiating your contract. The bonus spots are usually run during the off-peak hours.

Before you decide on a monetary amount per spot, be sure to check the rate card. This will show you the station's standard rates, which may be negotiable. You have your maximum negotiating power when you are a new account, so take advantage of it! This will set the tone for what will hopefully be a long, prosperous business relationship. Be as educated as possible to protect your company from learning lessons the hard way.

Once the contract is signed, you will get a copy for your files. Be sure to maintain all correspondence with each account. Your airing schedule will probably be included with your contract. This will verify when your spots or print ads will run. You can check the airing schedule against the run schedule you will get with your billing statement. It will be a notarized schedule documenting that your spots ran on television or radio. With print, your verification will come in the form of a copy of the ad run. Be sure to monitor your run schedules. If there is a discrepancy, contact your rep. He or she can do one of two things: credit your account for the ads that did not air, or run "make goods." (If the latter is done, you can request double the schedule. This will help ensure it doesn't happen again.)

Good media reps are invaluable to you and your success. They will do a lot of research and footwork for you. Once you have established yourself as a client, they will do everything they can to make sure you are happy. Because reps work almost exclusively by commission, they are highly motivated to retain you as their client. You will be continually updated on the ratings (the percentage of people who hear, see, or read your message at a given time). You will also be notified by your rep if the company is running special rates.

If by some chance, you really don't see eye to eye with your rep, or your philosophies just don't mesh, then you can call the sales manager and request a new rep. It is always best to avoid this situation if possible, but if there is just no way you can work with the rep and you don't want to switch stations, ask for someone else to handle your account.

Once you start advertising, reps from other companies will hear or see your ads and solicit you for advertising. Most reps "surf" radio and television stations looking for potential new clients. Be ready for this to happen, because it will. It is okay to hear their presentation. This will help you compile a file for possible advertising avenues. As another option, instead of meeting with each rep when requested, ask him or her to mail you an information packet about the company. Most will gladly do this. It is a terrific time-saver, and gives you good reference material. (Be sure and ask them to include a rate card.)

Contract Negotiations

Contracts are necessary to protect both the person buying advertising and the person selling advertising. Coming to a contract agreement takes the guess work out of your monthly expenditures and makes clear expectations for services. There is an art to negotiating contracts. The main thing you need to prepare for is making certain the services you are requesting are included in the contract. Once the details are laid out, the finances must be addressed. Each station (be it radio or television) and newspaper have what is called a "rate card." This card shows what the rates are for time in radio, television, or column inches in print, plus all the additional things you may have to pay extra for such as color, number of ad runs, and any discounts. Often, companies will agree to 10% to 15% less than what is on the rate card. If the amount of the service still seems too high to you, see if you can get more services listed without raising the cost. This allows for more value for you as the client. Suppose you are placing an ad in your local newspaper, and the cost is higher than you had budgeted for. Ask them if they will add color, go a few inches larger, or give you another run at no additional cost. Many companies are willing to negotiate these kinds of compromises. Often the rep is allowed to make these decisions. You can also get a better rate in a lot of cases if you commit to purchase a certain level of advertising or agree to run ads for 12 months. If you decide to sign this type of commitment, make sure there is an escape clause. This will allow you to cancel the agreement if the need arises.

Tailoring Your Marketing Strategies

Whether laying out your marketing plans quarterly, biannually, or annually, you must have specific goals in mind. They may be to increase your new patient base, to beef up your cataract surgery schedule, to integrate a new service into your practice, or any other target goal. The goal needs to be laid out so you can be very direct in your advertising. It is much more effective to stick to one or two goals at a time. The general public will hear your message and you want to be sure that they link the message to your name. If you have too much going on at one time, your message can easily get lost, and the busy consumer will tune you out. Let's look at a sample marketing plan.

Your practice has just acquired a new laser. This laser can do many things such as remove tattoos, age spots, flat benign lesions, sun spots, birthmarks, and freckles. A broad age group would have an interest or need for this type of laser. Before you market this laser, be certain that all the internal requirements are in place: the staff is trained, the paperwork is ready (such as consents, brochures, etc.), and all employees are aware of the advertisements (hopefully they have even had the opportunity to preview the ad materials).

Now you're ready to plan where to place the ads. The first item that is important to know is: Who is your audience? The target audience will range from older patients who would like to have the age spots removed from the back of the hands, to the teen who went through a rebellion and got a tattoo, to a toddler with a facial birthmark. In this case, your audience is virtually all ages. Second, what income level would the potential patient need to have? This would be considered a cosmetic procedure that insurance most likely would not pay, so the patient base you need to pull from would be those who have some disposable income. Third, would the patients you are looking for have some similar hobbies? When considering age spot removal, you would target active people from about age 45 and older. You'd target ages 18 to 45 for freckle removal. Birthmark removal could attract calls from parents of very young children and adults, so you see that the target groups are varied.

This is a good time to contact your media rep for demographic information. Demographics are a broad covering of various social and economic characteristics of a group of households or individuals. Some of the information that may be covered includes the number of people in a household, who is the head of the household, the occupation one holds, one's income level, whether one is a home owner or renter, one's hobby, one's age, etc. Your reps can help you obtain this type of specific information. (Remember, all of this statistical information is helpful, but there is no substitute for knowing the services and products you are promoting.)

After you have chosen your media (there will probably be more than one), you are ready to work on the "creative." This will include the ad copy—the ad text, photographs, graphics, television footage, radio jingles, or any other vehicles you choose to create your ad in order to get your message across as easily as you can. Then you can lay out the print ads, cut the voice copy for radio, and edit the television spots. (I'll guess that you had no idea how much fun you can have preparing media ads!) Once your media approach has been approved, it is ready to air. Time to sit back and watch the results happen—listen to the phones start to ring!

Figure 2-1. Sample ad.

The Media

Let's go over some of the many different media vehicles there are for you to use:

- Print ads: includes newspaper ads, magazines, and display ads for programs (high school year books, programs for community concerts, etc.)
- Radio: 30-second or 60-second ads (can produce customized jingles)
- Television: 30-second, 60-second, or 30-minute productions
- Yellow pages in the telephone book (this needs to be done even if you don't advertise anywhere else!)
- Newsletter: can be distributed to your mailing list, through the newspaper, or you can buy mailing lists
- Billboards: can be bought through outdoor advertising vendors
- Local talk shows: can be booked through your television rep for that station
- Network news programs that produce a medical segment (Call and ask for the editor that handles the program and present your subject idea. They always welcome new ideas for their programs)

Print Ads

There are many different approaches to presenting your ad. An approach that seems to be effective is "less is best." By this I mean that the eye will be drawn to the simplicity of an ad that is well-balanced. A good rule of thumb for print ads is to dedicate one-third to a photograph or graphics to accentuate your idea, use one-third for the written message, and leave the final third as open space (Figure 2-1). This creates an open, simple ad in the midst of what is often a crowded, busy paper. Your idea will shine through. Print ads require a conscious decision by the reader to take the time to read it. Think about it; many ads simply get glanced over without the least bit of consideration to their content. This is why a direct, simple approach is so effective. It will draw the reader to its message.

Radio

Radio ads have a more captive audience than print ads. Many listeners will tolerate hearing several commercial spots before tuning out or turning the dial. Studies also show that the highest percentage of listeners hear the first couple of ads after the music has stopped. What pushes that rate even higher is if you have music, or a singing "jingle," at the beginning of your message. This sort of "tricks" the listener into thinking they are about to hear music instead of a commercial and they remain attentive. Your advertising representative can assist you in putting together your ad, and you can even be the voice "talent" on your message if you'd like. Patient testimonials are also a positive way to get your message across, and your patients will be flattered to be chosen to speak about their experience on your behalf. Just the opportunity to do something different and fun keeps your patients talking about your practice. People like to hear others who have gone through the same procedure or exam that they are thinking of having. If you have provided a service to a well-known person in your community and that person is willing to provide a testimonial, that too is a great plus.

Radio is a great way to advertise because it is relatively inexpensive for the exposure you get, and it is economical to change the ads. Most radio stations make the tape for your commercial at no additional charge, and it can be changed any time. This is especially helpful to a practice that adds services on a regular basis, or is increasing its professional staff.

Remember, when you are choosing a radio station, the station's rating is more important than whether you like their particular style of music. It is not uncommon to make the mistake of only advertising on the stations you personally prefer. While this may work for some people, it is not the most effective way of choosing a station. Another way to choose stations is to pay attention to the music that is being played on store speakers while you are shopping. If you come across one particular station that seems to be prevalent, it may be a great place to start.

Television

Television is a whole new approach apart from print and radio. Here you are combining both a visual and an audio message. This is an avenue that can really help you develop the image you want to achieve. There is an entire spectrum of opportunities with television advertising. You can go plain or fancy. In some markets there are "blab talk" television stations where just about anyone can talk for 30 minutes about whatever they want to. Or you can go into full-blown production and produce a program on a weekly, monthly, or quarterly basis. Whichever avenue you choose, make sure the message you are sending out is one that not only informs and educates your audience, but also sets the stage for establishing credibility for your provider and your practice. Above all, make sure your delivery is honest, and that you don't overstate any provider's or procedure's ability beyond what it actually is.

Yellow Pages

Yellow page ads are a must for your practice even if you choose not to advertise by any other method. This will provide your community with a way to find you. It is a very acceptable, conservative way to promote your practice. Follow the same guidelines given previously in this chapter for print ads. If you choose a display ad, it is much more eye-catching if you use another color such as red or blue to outline or highlight your ad. Your yellow page rep can assist you with ad layout and other special details that can be added to enhance your display.

Telephone

Your telephone is another great source of advertising. When a patient gets put on hold in your office, is he or she listening to a dead line? Is he or she listening to a radio station that is hooked in (listening to someone else's advertising)? You can try using an on-hold company that compiles a continuous play tape and hooks it into your telephone lines. It is a wonderful way to inform your patients of the services your practice offers, update them on new surgical techniques, advise them of optical specials, or whatever you desire to share with your callers. Just imagine answering a call that has been on hold, and the caller requests an appointment for a consult to hear more about something he or she heard while being on hold. This is a very affordable way to advertise.

Other Options

As your advertising campaign becomes established, you will no doubt get requests from a lot of nonprofit organizations, school students, churches, and other special interest groups who are soliciting for ads. These are all worthy causes, but you will find that there are only so many resources to donate. Most of these opportunities are considered "dead ads" because they end up stuck in a program or school yearbook, and are not usually very productive in bringing in new patients to your practice. Consider these ads carefully. If it is an organization or school you have chosen to support because of your personal preference, then go ahead. Otherwise, it is usually best to pass these opportunities by. It is always a great thing to commit some percentage of your budget to support your community. Some favorites are: hospice, Older American's Council, American Cancer Society, Community Concert Association, etc. There are endless opportunities to make such donations.

Brochures are an excellent way to inform and promote your practice. If you have a customized brochure printed, it can be mailed out to all new patients coming into your practice along with a welcome letter (Figure 3-1). Its contents need to include the broad spectrum of services that your practice offers. The staff can take the brochures with them to public speaking engagements as well.

Press releases are valuable tools that keep the community updated on your practice and its staff. Any time your practitioners or staff members attend a continuing education program, or you have new equipment added to your office, inform the public about it. People love to read about their doctor. Patients also like to know that their doctor is keeping up with the fast-paced changes in medical care.

Newsletters can also be helpful in keeping your current patients informed. With today's computer capabilities, you can even do this in-house with the proper program. Mailing lists can be purchased so you can reach other potential patients. An even more economic avenue for distributing your newsletter is as an insert in your local newspaper(s). This does not require the purchase of a mailing list, and you pay one flat fee for the insertion and delivery of your newsletter.

Outdoor billboards can be leased on a monthly basis or longer. This avenue has become acceptable in most areas for marketing optical retail, and is slowly being used in medical arenas. Use discretion when considering this avenue of advertising.

Internal marketing can be just as important, if not more important, than external marketing. For the most part, the staff is the first contact your patients make with your practice. The staff members are valuable marketers in their own right. If you have patients coming in with saggy eyelids and your staff tells them their insurance might help pay to correct it, they begin to consider the possibility. If your myopic patients are having "fits" with their contact lenses and hate glasses, they may find that refractive surgery is the perfect solution to their frustrations. Having an observant, well-informed staff is invaluable. Sometimes all it takes is a casual mention of a procedure to generate patient interest. It is in your best interest to make sure your staff—from the receptionist through the most experienced clinician in your practice—is up to date on all the services your practice offers. This can be done through an in-office newsletter, office staff meetings, or any other way you choose to keep your staff informed. But they must be informed to be the most effective!

Public speaking gives your practice a high profile in your community and adds to its credibility as a health care provider. There are so many opportunities to provide this service. Some groups that are constantly looking for speakers include Lion's clubs, Rotary clubs, senior citizen's groups, the American Association of Retired Persons, the list could go on and on. The Chamber of Commerce in your community usually has a listing of all the civic organizations in the surrounding area. From there, contact each club president and offer your name and practice as a resource to provide a program for one of their meetings. Tailor your talks to the group's needs. The Lion's clubs enjoy hearing about anything from eye banking to what happens to the glasses they collect. Most seniors love to hear about plastic surgery, cataracts, diabetic retinopathy, etc. Rotary clubs are a perfect audience for refractive surgery. An additional bonus to these meeting presentations is that often your photo is sent to the paper, identifying you as the featured speaker for that meeting. Many patients come into practices because of doctors showing an interest in informing these type of groups. The school systems are always looking for speakers to present to their classes. Science and technology classes are the most commonly requested in our area, but these could differ from place to place. Just call the instructional coordinators of your school system and offer your practice as a resource for speakers. Members of the technical staff can go in many of these cases if scheduling doesn't allow a doctor to be there in person.

As you can tell, there is much more to marketing than meets the eye and ear. Much goes on behind the scenes. If you do your homework, you can have a very successful marketing campaign. This is simply a general guideline to help you get started. The best teacher with marketing is experience—find out what works for you. Don't be afraid to experiment.

Is It Worth It?

Tracking your marketing success can be done in several ways. Consider a separate telephone line dedicated only to your marketing. When you place an ad, list the special marketing phone number. This way you know without a doubt the call was generated by your advertising.

You may simply ask patients how they heard about your practice. This can be done at the time the appointment is made, or included as a question on the new patient information form filled out at the initial visit to your office.

Using a patient survey can also be a useful tool in tracking your marketing success. You can list all the avenues used such as specific radio or television stations, or newspapers. Also ask if a patient was referred by a friend or family member, or saw a yellow page ad.

Marketing often has a pyramid effect. First, potential patients see an ad in the paper, then they hear someone talking about your practice, then they hear a radio or television ad. The next thing you know, they're calling you when they need eyecare because their "automatic recall" came up with your name. Generally speaking, you need to run your campaign for a minimum of 3 months. This allows the patient time to hear your message and act on it. If you cannot afford to dedicate the resources required for a 3-month stint, you would be better served to delay your campaign awhile. Advertising for short spurts is the same as throwing your money away, so don't do it!

Once you have decided to take the advertising plunge, it is important that you don't disappear from the public eye. While the initial thrust of your advertising will be extensive, as the community becomes aware of your practice you can slow down the amount of advertising you do. Above all, have fun with it!

Patient Management

- If your patients are not treated well by your practice, they will find someone else who will treat them well, and they'll tell everyone they know to do the same.

- Do your best to render accurate information that is within your training.

- Your warm touch or smile may be the only one your patient gets all day.

- Look at your patients as whole people instead of "a cataract" or some type of case. This will enable you to treat them with the respect and dignity they deserve.

Patient Handling

The way that patient care is delivered can make or break a practice. It doesn't matter how successful your marketing program is at bringing patients to your door. If patients are not treated well, receiving a high level of care, not only will they find someone else to take care of their eyes, they'll tell everyone they know to do the same.

From the first contact a patient makes with your office, by telephone or in-person, your practice is being evaluated by the patient. This means that first impressions are vital to getting started on the right foot.

Let's begin at the door (literally). Door frames tend to get dirty because of heavy usage. Make certain cleaning this area is included in the day-to-day maintenance of your clinic. Once inside, have locations for patients to dispose of their used tissues. Check the area periodically and straighten magazines throughout the day. Don't forget to check other patient areas such as rest rooms as well.

An aquarium is very soothing to have in your reception area (notice the absence of the words "waiting room"). If you integrate an aquarium into your decor, be sure to establish who will provide for its upkeep before it is installed. Many pet stores will provide this service at a reasonable fee. If you have live plants in your office, they need to be well-watered and the dead foliage needs to be removed regularly. All these elements show that your practice is a stickler for detail, and your patients will love it. If you are not able to dedicate yourself to these kinds of details, switch to silk plants, and have plenty of magazine racks (to keep them off the table tops).

Handling the Telephone

Contacts by telephone are usually your initial opportunity to imprint a positive first impression. Vocal tones, background noise, and the length of time taken to answer the telephone all contribute to whether the first experience is a good one for your patient. A super way to "rate" your telephone secretary is to ask him or her to use a tape recorder and record several phone conversations. Then use the recording to evaluate vocal intonation, catch speech glitches (such as "umm" and "okay"), and evaluate effectiveness at answering questions. This is a great method for other staff members to evaluate themselves on their telephone technique as well.

The general rule for answering the telephone is that after two rings, the caller begins to get impatient. Answering the telephone with a smile on your lips transfers that smile right through the telephone line. A pleasant, helpful voice can calm and soothe a patient in the most grumpy mood. When booking appointments for your patients, assess how urgent the need is for the appointment, and also ask questions to evaluate how much time will be required with the practitioner. Remember to ask your new patients if they need directions to your office, and have a map drawn up to mail to them if needed.

If you cannot avoid putting a patient on hold, have something for them to listen to on the line. (Preferably, a customized on-hold service, but if radio is all you have, it is better than silence.) Keep patients on hold for the bare minimum amount of time. It seems that in our generation of impatience and hurry, the art of serving others is getting lost.

Do your best to render information that is within your training to handle. Often in our desire to help someone we can overstep our knowledge and give out incorrect information. This could decrease the confidence level that your patient has for your practice, or even worse, could actu-

September 9, 1996

Eyesight Associates
PO Pox 6479 216 Corder Road
Warner Robins, GA 31095

Patient's name   Account #:11
Patient's address
City, State zip code

Dear Patient:

I wanted to take the opportunity to welcome you to our practice and to offer assistance in making your visit a comfortable one.

I would appreciate it if you would complete the enclosed patient information sheet and bring it with you on the date of your appointment. This will alleviate some of your wait time.

All charges are due at the time of service unless your vision care is covered by your insurance company. We accept cash, check, American Express, Master Card, Visa, Pulsecard, and Discover.

Although we file and participate with many insurance companies, annual vision exams are not covered by most companies. Before the day of your appointment you should call your insurance company to verify that the provider you are scheduled to see and the services you are having are covered by them. Please check your policy manual carefully for physician and vision coverage.

Please bring in any medical or vision forms that may be required by your insurance company.

We ask that you pay copayments, noncovered services, and any unmet deductable amounts at the time of service. If we file your insurance and they have not paid within 45 days, the balance will automatically be transferred to your responsibility. Our new patient exams are $58.00 and could run up to $135.00 for a contact lens exam. Your fee will depend on the type of exam you have. If you cannot make this payment at the time of service, we ask that you make payment arrangements with our Patient Accounts Representatives, the day of your appointment.

If you need additional directions to our office or if we can be of further assistance, please do not hesitate to contact us at 1-912-923-5872. Again, welcome to Eyesight Associates.

Most sincerely,
Dr. I. C. Yew

Figure 3-1. Sample "welcome to our practice" letter.

ally harm the patient. To minimize the risk of offering incorrect information, be liberal with your questions to other members of your staff as you learn.

Once the appointment has been set, a telephone call a day ahead of the scheduled appointment is usually appreciated. This will also help reduce the occurrence of no-shows. In the event that a patient on the schedule is new, it can be helpful to send a "welcome to our practice" letter (Figure 3-1) along with the necessary patient information forms. Patients can fill these out at their leisure, and it often saves time once they have arrived at the office. Also include directions or a map to the office.

Telephone Triage

Having guidelines for taking incoming calls is helpful. Each practice is unique in its patient flow, and your doctor's input can be invaluable in compiling your guidelines. Write protocols for what to do in as many telephone situations as you can identify, including emergencies as a result of trauma, infections, and retinal detachments, plus the patient that is unhappy with a situation that occurred in your office.

Having a manual on your desk to refer to when a patient calls in with an emergency can sometimes make a tremendous difference in a patient's visual recovery following certain types of accidents. If a patient calls in and has had chemicals splashed in his or her eyes, you can look up the emergency protocol and read it to them over the phone. This way the chemical can be rinsed for the recommended time before the patient leaves to come to the office. This can be vital in preserving the cornea. There are many different situations that need to be handled properly to ensure the best outcome following an injury. The best way to handle any of those situations is to be prepared before the call comes in.

Patient Check-In

When your patients arrive for their appointment, they will know how to find your practice, and have the forms with them, thanks to the welcome letter (Figure 3-1) they received from your office. Hopefully the letter also reminded them to bring their insurance card(s) and medication(s). As they walk in, seeing an orderly reception room and a smiling receptionist is all they will need to solidify the positive first impression that you have worked so hard to achieve, plus it may help them to feel less apprehensive about their visit.

Patient waiting time can be a real thorn in the side of any practice. Patients have almost accepted the fact that a visit to the doctor will include a lengthy wait. If scheduling can be managed to minimize a patient's wait in your office, just imagine the positive public relations that can be derived! If a delay has occurred in the office, inform the patients that are waiting. Offer to reappoint to another time if they find it inconvenient to have to wait while the provider handles the situation that has caused the holdup.

The time has arrived to take the patient back to the eye lane. When calling your patient from the reception room, eye contact and a smile are always in order. If your patient needs a hand to help steady them, offer it. (As a general rule, geriatric patients like the caring touch that is offered. Patients who are in their more active stages in life usually don't.) Health care professionals have a unique opportunity to make a positive difference in a person's day. Treat your patients with dignity and care. Your warm touch or smile may be the only one your patient gets all day.

The Irate or Difficult Patient

Patients who become irate feel either insulted or hurt in some way. (It might even have been something that happened before they arrived at your office.) It may fall to you to smooth those ruffled feathers. One of the best ways to do that is to listen. Not just to hear, but really to listen to your patient. Try to listen objectively, not defensively. The patient's concern is rarely a personal attack. Pay particular attention to the last thing your patient says. It's usually the issue that is the greatest concern to him or her. Some patients will come in with a list of irritations. Address each one of them to the best of your ability.

If the patient is verbally upset and around other patients, it is best to direct him or her to a quiet out-of-the way spot where others won't be disturbed. On rare occasions a patient may be verbally abusive. If this happens, simply excuse yourself from the patient's presence and let the doctor or office manager handle the situation.

If a patient calls after having an encounter with your practice and is angry about some injustice or unhappy about the care received, be sure to give him or her your name. This gives the patient a sense of having an advocate in the office. Listen to the patient and repeat back what you understood him or her to say. Assure the patient that you will speak with whomever you need to in order to right the wrong. Then take action and call the patient back. This can diffuse the most unpleasant of situations. There are some patients that you will not be able to pacify, but always do your best. It helps to remember that even if the situation is one you have heard about many times over, it is probably the first time it has happened to this particular patient. Try to put yourself in his or her position and respond in the way you would like to be treated. As always, know your limitations. If the situation merits involvement from the administrator, or even the doctor, pass the details on and let them handle it. It is rare to come upon a situation that can't be handled by applying kindness and consideration.

Patient Safety

Create an environment that is free of potential hazards to your patients as they maneuver around in the office, both inside and out. Take a walk around the exterior of your building and observe the obstacles your patients must tackle before entering your door. If there are stairs, ramps, or uneven terrain, have them painted with high-contrast paint. Highlighting these areas will alert your patients to be cautious. This is especially helpful to patients with low vision or cataracts. When depth or color perception is compromised, it is easy to stumble on uneven pavement. If there are trees or shrubs close to walkways or doors keep them trimmed so the branches or leaves won't scrape against pedestrians. Provide a place for patients to dispose of their cigarettes before they enter the building. If you have a sign on the side of your building where there are walkways, make sure that the sign's edges are rounded and smooth so it won't scrape anyone's arms and shoulders or tear clothing.

Inside the doorways, place mats for patients to wipe their feet. Clean up wet areas on tiled floors right away. Eye lanes need to be well-lit when entering and exiting the room. If your examination chair has a foot platform, fold it up out of the patient's way as he or she gets in or out of the chair. Warn patients in advance if they are going to be seated on a chair that has wheels. If you are assisting blind or low-vision patients, have them rest their hand on your elbow or shoulder while you walk in front of them, describing any uneven flooring or turns they will have to maneuver.

Have the patient sit back if an adjustment is necessary in the positioning of equipment that their chin is resting on. Wipe all areas of instrument contact with alcohol or some other disinfecting solution. If you have a patient with a contagious disease such as chicken pox, isolate him or her from the rest of your staff and patients. If a patient has a potentially injurious accident while on office property, be sure to fill out an incident form (Form 11, Appendix, can be modified for patient accidents) and notify your supervisor.

Reporting Suspected Abuse

Reporting abuse is such a difficult thing to think about and act on when you are in a situation when you suspect that abuse may be taking place. The question "what if I'm wrong?" has probably stopped many people from reporting their suspicions. It may also keep a child in an abusive situation.

I can still recall the little girl's face, even though I saw her years ago for an eye injury. She was about the size of a petite 5 year old, though she was 8. Her eye injury was severe, and reportedly happened 3 days prior to her visit. Even on the third day after her injury, I could see what looked like the imprint of an extension cord on the surface of her cornea, accompanied by a hypopyon. She did not object in the least to being examined by slit lamp, though that bright light would have made most adults very uncomfortable. Her downcast gaze never lifted. The woman accompanying her spoke to the child with a harsh edge to her voice. Finally, the adult was asked to leave the room. Only then did this beautiful child give me a very brief, shy smile. I still wonder what happened to this little girl. I don't remember her name, but I'll never forget those eyes. I am sure that she was an abused child. If only I knew then what I know now about reporting abuse, maybe it could have made a small measure of difference in her life.

Health care professionals are mandated reporters of suspected abuse in many states. What this means is that we are required by law to report (or cause reports to be made) to the proper officials if we suspect that abuse has occurred. The person reporting does not have to *prove* the abuse has taken place. Because health care providers are mandated by law to report abuse, we are also protected by the law. We cannot be sued for reporting suspected abuse even if we are wrong. Check the laws in your state.

There are four primary types of abuse, each type displays its own set of symptoms: physical abuse, neglect, emotional/verbal abuse, and sexual abuse.

Physical Abuse

Physical abuse is any nonaccidental injury that is inflicted on another person. This can include severe beatings, burns, human bites, and broken bones. Ophthalmically, the most common sign of physical abuse is retinal hemorrhage. Direct blows to the eye may cause bruising and swelling, orbital fractures, subconjunctival hemorrhages, hyphema, dislocated lenses, and/or retinal detachments.

We need to be on alert when the story told by a caregiver doesn't match up with the physical injury we find on evaluation. Other strong indicators of physical abuse include: the explanation of the injury is not believable, the explanation is not consistent with any other information, there is a time lapse from the occurrence of the injury to when treatment is sought, the caretaker changes the story, there is a suspicion of previous abuse, the caretaker projects blame, or the caregiver overreacts to the child's misbehavior.

Neglect

Neglect is the withholding of, or failure to provide a person with basic necessities of life such as clothing, shelter, food, medical care, proper hygiene, adequate supervision, and general care. Symptoms of neglect include having inappropriate clothing for the weather and season, not bathing, having unkempt hair, and poor dental hygiene. Ophthalmic signs and symptoms of malnutrition can include external changes (lid swelling, a sensation of "fullness" in the eyes), dry eyes, decreased functioning of retinal cells (resulting in night blindness), optic atrophy, optic neuritis, and possibly a higher rate of cataract formation.

Emotional/Verbal Abuse

Emotional/verbal abuse is aggressive, excessive, or unreasonable demands on children or adults that is beyond their capability to perform. Insulting, belittling language is used to harshly scold or revile. The words of an abuser are aimed at tearing down or destroying self-image. Physical and emotional contact is withheld to the detriment of the person's normal emotional or physical development. Often times this type of behavior is witnessed in the doctors' office. Because this type of abuse causes scars on the inside, it can be more difficult to detect.

Sexual Abuse

Sexual abuse is the exploitation of a child for the sexual gratification of an adult or juvenile. This type of abuse can range from nontouching, to fondling, to intercourse. Abuse of this nature can be difficult to detect unless the victim talks to you about it. Ophthalmically, look for signs of physical abuse. Subconjunctival hemorrhages are common if the victim strains to resist (Valsalva's maneuver). Other symptoms you can look for include an advanced knowledge regarding sexual matters, sex play with dolls, promiscuous dressing or behavior, low self-esteem, withdrawal, lack of friends within the peer group, and imaginary friends.

Conclusion

Look at your patients as whole people instead of "a cataract" or some other case. This will enable you to treat them with the respect and dignity they deserve. If your office as a whole can achieve this one thing, you will have record numbers of patients come through your door. I am not a believer of the old adage "Oh well, you can't please everyone." This is a convenient way of accepting that, as health care providers, we have failed to meet the needs of a patient. I do believe that if each patient is heard and his or her needs assessed and met, you will find your job more rewarding that you ever thought possible.

Chapter 4

Office Finances

KEY POINTS

- Accounts Receivable represent monies owed and are not spendable until they are collected.

- One of the best billing methods is cycle billing where one fourth of the statements are mailed every week.

- The secret to proper collection is to follow protocol and not allow the Accounts Receivable to age more than necessary.

- Health insurance is a private contract between the patient and the insurance company.

Accounting systems can be either manual or electronic. While manual systems such as the peg-board are workable, they are labor intensive. For example, most peg-board systems require a gymnastic effort to generate daily and monthly Accounts Receivable figures. They are cumbersome and allow only one person to work on them at a time.

In contrast, computerized accounting systems can have simultaneous access by many staff members and still input the data correctly. With computerized accounting systems, the numbers are automatically placed into their proper categories and ready for organization into a report. Of the many types of reporting structures a computer can generate, here are a few of the most important:

1. A report showing current Receivables by payer should be generated and tracked every 6 months. The intent is to establish patterns of payment, if any, from all of your payers, such as the third-party folks. The purpose of this is to serve as a list for action items (items that demand special attention) when you have problems with carriers and/or payment. For example: Each type of problem would have an action item related to a specific goal or objective that solves the problem. In this way, you will be able to track your third-party involvements and see if they are really worth continuing the next time the contract is due.

2. A report showing current Receivables by procedure is done so that the physician can determine which type of procedures are most likely to generate long term Receivables. This is intended to enable the staff to take preventative measures on items that have been routinely denied.

3. An alphabetized list of private payer contracts (health maintenance organizations [HMOs], preferred provider organizations, etc.), should be maintained in order to be able to gauge payment policy for claims. The practice should list all of these different payer contracts by carrier and delineate special requirements such as "needs referral from primary care physician."

4. A report of the Accounts Receivable aged into 30-, 60-, 90-, and 120-day categories and rearranged in descending order are shown in Table 4-1. By arranging the Accounts Receivable in descending order, the staff can begin collecting on the accounts that have the largest outstanding amounts.

Accounts Receivable

The winning philosophy with regard to office finances is to understand the concept of Accounts Receivable. Accounts Receivable represent monies owed and are not spendable until they are collected. The good news about Accounts Receivable is that it is money owed to the practice. The bad news is that it is usually tomorrow's money. The time value of money decreases with the length of time it takes to be collected. If, for example, the practice was owed $50,000 in Accounts Receivables and it wished to purchase $50,000 worth of equipment or instrumentation, it would either have to borrow the money from itself or from a lending institution. Thus, the bank would charge interest and the $50,000, which is now due the practice, is actually worth less because of the practice having to expend additional monies in interest payments to the bank while waiting for the original money to arrive. If the practice had the $50,000 in the bank, it could be collecting interest on it. Therefore, not having the financial vehicle to invest now reduces the potential value of the outstanding Receivable even more. In today's modern independent eyecare practitioner's office, cash is king.

Table 4-1.
Sample Computer Printout For Accounts Receivable Practice Aging Totals By Payer For All Doctors At All Offices

Balance Greater Than $0	Outstanding Totals/% of Outstanding Total					
	Balance Older Than 30 Days (Includes Credit Balances)					
Responsible Party	0–30 days	31–60 days	61–90 days	91–120 days	more than 120 days	Total
Miscellaneous Insurance	25.51 1%	0.00	46.57 1%	4254.43 87%	587.51 12%	4914.02 1%
Patient	31538.24 22%	24679.89 17%	13521.27 10%	7111.16 5%	64780.66 46%	141631.22 43%
Other Insurance	0.00	0.00	80.00 15%	0.00	459.43 85%	539.43 0%
Medicare	52812.15 33%	12451.44 8%	784.00 0%	667.82 0%	92988.40 58%	159703.81 48%
Ohio Department of Human Services	5932.76 53%	3350.07 30%	652.15 6%	540.26 5%	754.52 7%	11229.76 3%
Community Mutual	0.00 100%	0.00	0.00	0.00	26.32	26.32 0%
Aetna Columbus	847.52 100%	0.00	0.00	0.00	0.00	847.52 0%
Aetna Life Ins Co	222.15 95%	0.00	0.00	11.04 5%	0.00	233.19 0%
Central Beneficial	14.28 100%	0.00	0.00	0.00	0.00	14.28 0%
Bureau of Workmen's Compensation	300.00 9%	370.00 11%	680.00 20%	315.00 9%	1670.60 50%	3335.60 1%
Travelers Medica	0.00	7170.00 95%	160.00 2%	197.70 3%	0.00	7527.70 2%
American Association of Retired Persons	1055.76 100%	0.00	0.00	0.00	0.00	1055.76 0%
Community Mutual	1239.22 99%	0.00	17.10 1%	0.00	0.00	1256.32 0%
Goodyear	33.99 100%	0.00	0.00	0.00	0.00	33.99 0%
United American	26.08 100%	0.00	0.00	0.00	0.00	26.08 0%
Comm Mutual/ Automotive	232.41 89%	0.00	0.00	0.00	30.00 11%	262.41 0%
Self Insured	0.00	195.00 100%	0.00	0.00	0.00	195.00 0%
Totals	94306.39 28%	48216.40 14%	15941.09 5%	13097.41 4%	161271.12 48%	332832.41 100%

Accounts Payable

Accounts payable represents the money owed by the practice to others: suppliers, instrument companies, the post office, the bug exterminator, etc. Creditors can be listed alphabetically or by account number. Every credit purchase and incoming bill must be posted. In addition to recording cash payments, be sure to deduct any returns (check with your supplier for their policy on this), payments, and credits. As payments are made they are logged as cash disbursements. In cases where the practice develops a debit balance (overpayment), this can be flagged by using parentheses or some other mark. Obviously this is all handled most easily by computer, which can generate printouts and other pertinent reports. It could be done on a simple spread sheet, or a special accounting program can be used.

Billing

The secret to good billing habits revolves around consistently advising patients as to their status. One of the best methods is to use cycle billing in which statements from the practice are mailed every single week rather than at the end of the month. This method simply breaks up the alphabet into four sections. For example: Week 1 is used to mail bills to all patients whose last names begin with A through F; week 2 is used to bill G through L; in week 3 bill M through S; and in week 4 bill T through Z. In this manner the financial pipeline will remain full.

Collecting

It is the eyecare team's job to maximize income and minimize Accounts Receivable. The secret to proper collection is following an established office protocol and not allowing the Accounts Receivable to age more than necessary. The basic rules for achieving these are as follows:

1. Collect all patient responsible fee for service and any patient co-pays at the time of the visit.
2. Collect all noncontractual insurances in which the office does not participate. For example: The patient with Medicare as a primary insurance and a secondary, or supplementary, insurance in which the practice does not participate, would be required to pay the 20% of the Medicare allowed amount.
3. Collect all fees for all noncontractual optical devices (spectacles and contact lenses) at the time the patient receives them.

Asking the patient for money may seem awkward, but it shouldn't be. The physician and staff have provided a service to the patient and have a right to expect to be reimbursed for that service. Here are several scripts you can use to help with collections:

Previsitation Coverage Script

This script is to be used when calling patients to verify the coordination of insurance benefits prior to the office visit.

Staff member: "Hello, this is _______ from _______________, the office of Dr. _________. In order to save you time during your visit, Dr. _________ was wondering what coverage or insurance plan you will be using on _______ (say the day of the week). Do you have a few minutes now to discuss this?"

If yes, then proceed to verify coverage. If no, then offer to call the patient back at a more convenient time.

Noncontractual Supplementary Insurance Script

"Mr./Mrs. __________, Dr. __________ accepts insurance assignment for your primary carrier (Medicare). As you remember, Medicare pays 80% of an allowed amount. This is called the allowable, in your case $ _______. The 20% difference may be paid by your supplemental (secondary) insurance. Because this policy is a private contract between you and your supplemental insurance company, the responsibility of this 20% therefore belongs to you. Our office will be happy to file it for you and have the check come directly to you. Or we can wait 30 to 45 days for the payment. But if it takes longer or there is a claim problem, we will transfer the claim to you. Is that okay?"

Script for the Good-bye Desk, Checkout, or Cashier

"Mr./Mrs. __________, all of your papers seem to be in order. Are there any questions we can answer before completing this visit?"

"The fee for today is only $_______, which represents (choose one):
1. The doctor's total fee.
2. The noncovered insurance portion (refraction).
3. The doctor's nonallowed portion.
4. A noncontractual insurance that the office does not accept.

The remainder will be billed for you. If you have any questions, please feel free to call ____________."

Script for Telephone Questions on Fees

Desk: "I'm glad you called. I'd be happy to tell you what our fees are but first, so I can give you a better idea of what they might be, I'd like to find out exactly why you'd like to see Dr. ____________."

or

Desk: "I can understand you're concerned about prices. With the economy the way it is, who can afford not to be concerned?"

Prospective Patient: "No one."

Desk: "Well, rest assured, we are very affordable. First of all, we accept most major insurance, as well as Visa and Mastercard. But, best of all, our fees are below average for our town.

"But, you're not going to choose your eye doctor based solely on price. We know that. The most important thing is to take good care of your eyes. Dr. ____________ has over _____ years of experience. What's more, he/she has helped over _________ people have great vision. Hardly anyone in town has that track record or nearly that much experience. He/She is a real expert in eye wear. That makes our fees an even better all-around value. I have an appointment available at _______ tomorrow or _______ the following day. Which is better for you?"

The collection portion of office finances also revolves around a good report generator that identifies the specifics of the amount outstanding. Typically, this is sorted into the following categories—Private, insurance only, HMO, etc. Within each category, the report generator should age these accounts in the following manner: 0–30, 30–60, 60–90, 90–120, and over 120 days (Table 4-1.).

Once the report has been generated, collection action can be taken as follows:
1. A secondary statement advising the patient that the amount is past due.
2. A follow-up phone call within 10 days of nonpayment.
3. An official office letter sent with a Return Receipt Requested.
4. Turn over to a professional collection agency.

Third Party (Insurance) Processing

It is the role of the eyecare staff to ensure that the coordination of insurance benefits is correct. In today's world of multiple third party payer varieties, identifying the payment coverage benefits (primary, secondary, etc.) remains one of the great challenges for eyecare practitioners.

With more and more independent eyecare practitioners becoming involved with Medicare as a secondary payment, it becomes important to understand exactly what rights you have and how Medicare actually computes or calculates your pay. Let's use the word calculate.

Carriers calculate your Medicare secondary payments in the same fashion whether claims are assigned or unassigned. Eligible practitioners can collect a combined amount equal to the third party payer's allowable charge if that charge is higher than the Medicare allowable. It is important to note that previously, physicians who accepted assignment couldn't collect more than the Medicare allowable amount from the combined payments of a primary payer and Medicare. That meant that independent practitioners had no incentive to bill a private insurer first!

For example: Assume a charge of $175 for treating a patient. The employer insurance allows $150 of the charge and pays 80% of that amount of $120; the Medicare fee schedule amount is only $125. To calculate the Medicare second payment, perform the following arithmetic:
A. Determine the Medicare payment (80% of $125 = $100)
B. Subtract the employer plan allowable charge from the employer plan's payment ($150 - $120 = $30) The employer plan allowable charge of $150 is higher than the Medicare fee schedule amount of $125. Therefore,
C. The Part B carrier, Medicare, pays $30.

What The Patient Needs To Know

- Bring all insurance cards with you to every visit.

- Understand that health care insurance is a private contract between you and the insurance company, not between the insurance company and your doctor.

- There is a difference between what insurance pays and what insurance allows.

- Remember that some procedures may not be covered by your insurance carrier at all.

- Some of your services may require a second opinion before insurance will approve payment.

- Your primary insurance carrier *must* be billed first and after they respond, your secondary insurance may then be filed.

Table 4-2.

Sample Insurance Coverage Matrix
Check Out Quick Reference

Insurance	Medical Diagnosis a Must	If Refractive Only	Bill Extended	Any Co-pay	Testing Co-pay	Authorization Required	Next Visit Authorization	Bill Consult First Visit	Collect On Deductible	If We Refer to Specialist	Other Information
1199	yes	voucher/ must collect	yes	no	no	none	none if medical	no	no	N/A	1199 for each visit
Aetna	no	okay	no	yes	no	referral/or every 2 years	referral	yes	no	go to PCP	every 2 years no referral
Aetna Select	no	okay	no	yes	no	PCP note on prescription pad	PCP referral necessary every visit	yes	no	go to PCP	
Blue Choice\ POS	yes	patient pays	yes	check card/ patient	no	authorization # or out of net	patient to PCP for next authorization	yes	no	to PCP or out of net	
Blue Choice	yes	patient pays	yes	check card/ patient	no	none	none	yes	no	N/A	
Choice Care HMO	yes-adults	okay/kids only	yes	yes	no	referral	referral	yes	no	go to PCP	check referral for number of visits
Choice Care	yes-adults	okay/kids only	yes	yes	no	encouraged	PCP authorization	yes	no	go to PCP	if not referred by PCP/full payment
Childcare of Lilco	yes-adults	okay/kids only	yes	yes	no	referral forms	referral	yes if PCP referred	no	go to PCP	retirees referral
Childcare of Suffolk	yes-adults	okay/kids only	yes	$8	$8 VF/FA	none	none	yes if MD required	no	patient to call	
Cigna HMO	no	okay	yes	yes	no	authorization number	patient gets from PCP	yes	no	patient to PCP	
Cigna POS	no	okay	yes	20%/$10 with authorization	no	encouraged	patient gets from PCP	yes-if PCP referred	$300	patient to get authorization	
Corporate Health	no	okay	no	check card	no	none	none	no	no	N/A	part of US Healthcare
Healthnet	no	1 year okay	no	none	none	referral form	check referral form	yes	no	patient to PCP	check referral for number of visits
JJ Newman	yes	patient pays	yes	yes-$8	yes/VF/FA	none	N/A	no	no	N/A	patient must fill out form

N/A = not applicable; PCP = primary care provider; POS = point of service; HMO = health maintenance organization; VF = visual field; FA = fluorescein angiogram; MD = medical doctor.

Third party vision care insurance varies greatly from program to program. It is the job of the eyecare staff to understand the different insurance types, along with the rules and regulations for their use. Coverage types are either contractual or noncontractual. They are either commercial or private. The best way for the practice to understand and implement these different programs is to create a worksheet with a matrix (Table 4-2). The matrix lists all third party insurance programs in which the office participates. This is usually done vertically on a page. Along the horizontal top, all the particular variations should be listed, such as patient must pay a co-pay, or patient is eligible only one time per year, or patient must have a referral. Computers are excellent for this type of work and should be used to the highest degree feasible.

OptA

Banking

Once payment has arrived at the office, a banking protocol should be adopted, as follows:
1. Deposit monies on a daily basis.
2. Provide bonding for those staff members who must handle money.
3. Avoid potential embezzlement by having one staff member handle the money collected (daily payments, check by mail, etc.) and a different staff member handle the accounting of these monies. For example: Monies collected for the day are totaled and the receipt of those totals are handed to another staff member who then posts those payments to the accounting ledger. In this manner, both staff members should balance the total by having the exact same amount that is collected as the amount that is posted.
4. When paying the office bills, always notate the specific purpose for the payment so that the practice's accountant can properly place the Payables in the appropriate categories.
5. An appropriate amount of money (cash) from the General Fund should be allotted for incidentals and is usually kept by one person in the office (receptionist) in a cash box or drawer. This cash is accounted for on a predetermined time basis (daily, weekly, or monthly). Incidentals could be described as office lunches when physicians cannot get away from the office, cash on delivery packages, etc. A Petty Cash form should be filled out when cash is used and reconciled against the balance remaining. At no time should persons other than the authorized caretaker be allowed to remove these monies.

Chapter 5

The Office Manager

KEY POINTS

- Job descriptions illustrate areas of responsibility. Protocols explain how to do a job.

- Keys to effective office meetings include conducting meetings on a regularly announced schedule, setting a starting *and* ending time, and use of a written meeting agenda.

- The rules for employment should be expressed in a comprehensive office policy manual.

- The key to a successful and dynamic staff is to hire as if you were casting for a play.

- "Discrimination" may be said to be legal if it is a standard for employment. Obtain counsel from a labor attorney to rule on questionable standards before they are applied.

- If one expects, one must inspect.

- Delegation is a key developer of people.

Duties of the Office Manager

Virtually every eyecare office has at least one person who is delegated additional authority to help the doctor run the practice. This authority varies from minimal responsibility to full responsibility with as many variations as there are eyecare professionals. The definition of an office manager can sometimes be elusive, yet it is important that this person have a clearly defined job description in order to succeed. As with all well-run eyecare offices, success is most easily attained when all members of the staff understand exactly what are their responsibilities and authorities.

Job Description

The job description for an office manager will usually read something like this:

The office manager shall have the overall managerial responsibility for personnel, facilities, management information systems, communications, interoffice systems development, contracting and marketing, and insurance benefits.

Job Description Analysis:

1. Personnel
   A. Determine present and forecast future personnel needs in the following areas:
      1. Front Office: Telephone, scheduling, records, cashier, etc.
      2. Back Office: Assisting, technology, diagnostics, surgical scheduling.
      3. Business: Insurance, collections, public relations, and marketing.
      4. The questions to ask are:
         a. What are the present office systems in place?
         b. Who currently performs these tasks and how well are they being performed?
   B. Develop job descriptions by listing all tasks each employee performs. Example: What are the primary, secondary, and tertiary authorities and responsibilities?
   C. Hire, manage, and discharge through an organized method of documentation including written office policy manual interpretation, frequent praising, counseling, and performance feedback. Recommend and effect job separation through supportive documentation and within appropriate governing medical/legal parameters.
   D. Establish salary levels based on the standards of the community, eyecare industry, seniority, and ability through reliable information.

2. Facilities (Internal)
Oversee all pertinent internal office needs. This includes, but is not limited to supplies, instrumentation, and equipment acquisition.
   A. Identify and supervise staff to meet the above needs.
   B. Identify and record inventory, warranties and guarantees, and implement an ongoing log of products and services, as well as maintenance resources.
   C. Predict future internal office needs to ensure an ongoing smoothly functioning office. Example: Copy machine needs replacement. Action: Research and bid at least three similar products before recommending a replacement.

3. Facilities (External)
Assess and determine the maintenance requirements such as trash, utilities, housekeeping, grounds, and emergency systems.
   A. Supervise and report the maintenance of these areas on a regularly scheduled basis.
   B. Project future requirements.

C. Prepare appropriate budgets for the above standard external facilities.

    4. Management Information Systems

Develop the data processing needs of the office.

A. Assess computer or computer-assisted needs.

B. Assist in the acquisition of hardware and software through analysis of need and, if necessary, through the use of consultants.

C. Forecast future data processing needs and report in a timely fashion. Example: Appointment scheduling or on-line charting.

5. Communications

A. Determine the status of current internal, as well as external, communication systems including telephone, paging, lighting, etc.

B. Develop orientation and ongoing training programs to facilitate improvement of personnel communication skills. Example: Full staff educational meetings and/or departmental meetings.

C. Forecast future communications requirements and develop appropriate budgets. Example: Staff picnics, retreats, in-house presentations, etc.

6. Intraoffice System Development

A. Develop a workable standard operating procedures manual to encompass all aspects of the eyecare professional's office.

B. Maintain and report reviews of such intraoffice systems to the eyecare professional and/or his or her staff on a periodic basis.

C. Hold regularly scheduled eyecare professional/office manager meetings to ensure ongoing executive communications. (Include written minutes.)

7. Contracts and Marketing

A. Assume overall responsibility for public relations and marketing through the acquisition of medical contracting knowledge. Example: Attend preferred provider organization and marketing seminars.

B. Develop an awareness of community activities relevant to the practice.

C. Seek knowledge of both private and public sector industry as it relates to eyecare services. Example: Industry health fairs or senior citizen programs.

8. Benefits

A. Develop an understanding of all employees' benefits, including group health, malpractice, personal liability, workers' compensation, and disability insurance.

B. Analyze and recommend appropriate companies, policies, and programs that meet the office philosophy regarding these benefits.

C. Control and maintain records and report status to appropriate personnel in a timely fashion.

D. Interface with other benefits professionals (including a certified public accountant or an attorney) regarding pension and/or profit sharing, etc. In general, the office manager should be the primary source of information flowing from the office to the eyecare professional. The nature of the information presented should be of high quality and would not require verification. It should be of sufficient latitude and carry with it, when appropriate, recommended courses of action.

No employee will continue to work at peak efficiency without knowledge of how he or she is doing. The office manager is no exception.

Protocols

Whereas job descriptions illustrate the areas of responsibility, protocols explain how to do the job. This is how the job description for office manager typically looks:

Position Objectives

Manage the staff in such a way as to offer patients complete satisfaction with the finest medical care, thereby building the practice, while also seeing that the practice will be capable of meeting the future demands with the most progressive care delivery system.

Primary Responsibilities

Performance Improvement

1. Develop and maintain results-oriented job descriptions for each job in the office.
2. Establish and maintain performance standards for each job.
3. Assist each staff member in their development with semiannual performance reviews.
4. Maintain a personnel file on each employee that reflects their performance on the job.
5. Develop and maintain a procedure manual that accurately reflects the agreed upon standard methodology of performing tasks within the office.

Development

6. Recruit and select all new employees.
7. Determine the training needs of all personnel.
8. Design on-the-job training means for new employees.
9. Ensure that all personnel are given the proper opportunity to learn the skills necessary to perform their job.
10. Ensure that sufficient cross-training is done or outside help is available so the loss of any one employee will not hamper office performance.
11. See that staff are given the first opportunity to fill all higher-level openings.

Communication

12. Monitor telephone techniques as well as staff/patient communication skills to ensure that patients are being handled in a responsive caring manner.
13. Conduct daily briefing sessions with the staff to review the day's schedule and any anticipated changes from the routine.
14. Conduct weekly staff meetings to review any problems presented during the previous week.
15. With the physician present, conduct monthly staff meetings to address future opportunities for improving the care delivery system in general.

Reward System

16. Determine all appropriate salary increases.
17. Develop and maintain a staff incentive plan based on the entire office's ability to improve performance as planned.
18. When and if appropriate, determine individual performance bonuses based on each individual's ability to meet and exceed job standards.

Feedback

19. Monitor staff morale to ensure that the physicians are advised of any impending personnel problems.

20. Keep the physicians advised of any problem that will affect the staff's ability to work to schedule or deliver the appropriate care.
21. Monitor patient attitude periodically to determine opportunities for improvement of the care delivery system.
22. Periodically monitor the staff's attitude, sharing results with all members during team-building sessions that contribute to overall office development through a better understanding on everyone's part.
23. Meet weekly with the managing partner and monthly with all physicians to report results and confirm directions.
24. Recommend to the physician any punitive action including termination, documenting all events that have led to one's recommendations.

Financial

25. Develop a 12-month budget for all expenditures, updating same on a periodic 3-month basis.
26. Monitor expenditures versus budget on a monthly basis and report any deviations to the managing partner or your superior.
27. Monitor the aging of Accounts Receivable to determine when collections move outside agreed-upon standards.
28. Reconcile cash collection at day's end and see that cash is properly deposited in the bank.
29. Monitor all inventories to ensure proper control.
30. Prepare an annual salary budget that anticipates the adjustments expected for each staff member.
31. Develop a yearly training budget reflecting the total costs of these activities.

Operational

32. See that descriptive literature is developed and available to aid the communication of proper information to all patients.
33. Counsel any patient disturbed by their treatment.
34. Interface with all sales representatives who do not have a pre-established appointment to determine if the representative's information would benefit the physicians or other staff members. If so, then schedule an appropriate time for such a meeting.
35. See that the overall appearance of the office is maintained.
36. Make sure that equipment is always functional and that supplies are always available to meet daily patient demands.
37. Coordinate all outside engagements for the physician.
38. Maintain and update the office policy manual as necessary.
39. Maintain a vacation schedule for physicians and staff and be sure to offer staff vacation days when the physician is away from the office.
40. Assist other staff members in the performance of their duty whenever appropriate and necessary to expedite patient flow.

Effective Authority

1. Award salary increases within the proper range and budget.
2. Convene staff meetings as necessary.
3. Assign staff responsibilities as appropriate to perform office services.

4. Recruit and select staff within the limits of an approved plan.

5. Issue written performance evaluations (following physician review) to the staff.

6. Take all appropriate leadership and disciplinary action short of termination to maintain control.

7. Recommend termination if necessary, to the managing partner.

8. Approve training courses or outside training assistance within the budget that will aid in overall staff development objectives.

The individual parts of this job description are measurable indicators that can be used to monitor success in each individual area.

Time Management for the Office Manager

In addition to the challenge of living up to, or exceeding, the standards for performing job responsibilities as laid down in the job description, good office management also demands the ability to be organized and control time.

Personal time management can best be controlled through the following guidelines:

1. *Handle paper only once.* Many practitioners allow paper and paper-based tasks to interfere with more important work. For example, they often stop in the midst of a project to review the daily mail by picking it up, shuffling the pieces, and becoming mesmerized in the process. Similarly, they put aside what they are already doing to peruse paperwork dropped on their desks by colleagues, only to add it to the ever-growing piles in their "in" baskets. Even worse, when faced with several telephone messages, they sit aimlessly, wondering who to call first while the clock ticks away.

Efficient professionals touch whatever paper they are handed only when they plan to file it, discard it, or act on it. They never handle the same piece of paper twice. Time management experts call this rule the "Three D" principle: when it comes to paper, do it immediately, delegate it, or drop it.

2. *Prioritize all tasks.* Each evening make a list of those tasks you must accomplish the following day, and others you would like to accomplish. Then divide a second sheet of paper into three columns. Let column one represent all jobs requiring completion at a specific juncture; column two, mandatory projects with no particular deadlines; and column three, matters you wish to handle eventually.

Assign all tasks on your original list to one of the three classifications, prioritizing within columns as you go along. With this accomplished, select just five items to act on. Do not set unrealistic goals for yourself by exceeding the limit; rather, save the remainder of the list for another day.

Next, consult your planning calendar and record estimated completion times for the five projects on your agenda. Schedule a sufficient number of hours or minutes for each task, beginning with the one you have deemed most important. The next day, at the appointed time, clear your desk and work on the first job until it is finished. Then handle the other four matters in order of importance.

Finally, when creating your task list, use different-colored pens to symbolize prioritized and nonprioritized items. For instance, you may want to indicate the most important projects you wish to handle in red ink, and other matters in blue ink. As a result, you will find it easier to "visualize" a proper position for each job within the structure of your three columns.

Just as significantly, when scheduling blocks of time for completing jobs outside the office, allow for "transition periods" and record them on your calendar as well. For example, if one of your priorities for the day is attending an 11 AM meeting that is 15 minutes away by car, your date book should read, "10:45 AM, leave for meeting." If you simply write, "11 AM meeting," you will be more likely to tolerate delays or distractions and fall irretrievably behind schedule.

3. *Organize with folders.* As an adjunct to your task priority list, use a filing system to organize your workdays. Once a month, create a folder for each day you intend to work during the next 30 days, and mark it accordingly (eg, "June 1," "June 2," etc.). As you plan your daily tasks, place all related data (eg, paperwork, phone numbers, notes, and forms) in the appropriate file. Review the contents of each folder the day before you actually use it. This way, when you are ready to work on a particular project slated for a certain day, you will know where to find its necessary components.

Here is one example of how a filing system works to your advantage: Suppose that on June 15 you receive an invitation to a seminar scheduled for July 10. Because registration for the session is due on July 5, you must mail your application form and fee by July 1. Consequently, you place the invitation in the file labeled "July 1."

On June 30, you pull the next day's folder and find the seminar form. You fill it out, attach a check, stamp an envelope, and place everything back where you found it. On July 1, you review the file again, find the envelope, and drop it in the mail. With the filing system in place, it is impossible to overlook such small details. Planning this way saves a good deal of time in the long run.

4. *Set "suspense dates."* To make prioritization and organization even easier, "suspense dates," or deadlines for task completion, should always be reviewed when issuing or receiving assignments. Accordingly, work-related requests should always be greeted with a response such as "Fine, when do you need it?" If no "real" deadline exists for a specific project, an informal "suspense date" can be issued by saying, "When I am finished, I will let you know!" This way you can avoid wasting time rectifying the mistakes so often inherent in last-minute "rush jobs."

5. *Limit telephone time.* Few things are more frustrating than shelving a project simply because the time you had allotted to it has been consumed by an overabundance of pointless telephone calls. However, there are two ways to cure "telephone tyranny."

For starters, end long, rambling phone conversations by interrupting yourself. Pause suddenly in the midst of making a point, then exclaim, "Oh, something important has come up! I'll speak with you later!"

Similarly, when placing telephone calls, never consent to remaining on "hold." Many eyecare professionals feel they can accomplish other tasks while waiting to be connected to another party, but doing so effectively is really impossible. Thus, if asked to hold, assert yourself by saying, "No, I cannot. This is ___________ and I wish my call to be put through now, please. Thank you." Should a receptionist place you on "hold" without your permission, hang up and try again later.

6. *Avoid long waits.* Never wait more than 15 minutes for anybody. Following this rule lets others know that time is important to you, and that you dislike wasting it. Deviate from this practice only for medical emergencies or in extenuating circumstances such as inclement weather.

7. *Control meetings.* This topic is covered in detail later in this chapter.

Handling Company Representatives

People who come into your practice representing other companies or products are most commonly referred to as "reps." They are liaisons between you and the firm or product they represent. Reps can be a valuable resource for your office. A good rep has a thorough knowledge of the product he or she represents and is willing to share that knowledge. Reps know a lot of people in their field, and often share information about their products with other reps. They are usually the first ones to know what's new on the market, and when it will be available.

Reps are a great resource to provide training sessions to your staff. They can teach your staff how to use and promote a product. If the product is pharmaceutical, the rep can teach you how the drug works, when it is the most effective, and other such useful information. He or she can also provide research material connected to the product.

Often reps will find themselves with some extra time while in your area and will drop in. If this only happens on rare occasions, it can be fit into your schedule. When it happens often, or on a busy day, and your doctor is already behind on his or her schedule, it can create some additional stress and put you further behind. It is best to request that your reps call in advance and set up an appointment. This way, you can block off time when needed. Drug reps are required to get the doctor's signature when leaving samples. When your schedule is tight, you can help by taking the form to the physician yourself instead of giving the rep access to your provider(s).

Reps have up-to-date information on what's new, and how to order products other than what they themselves carry, because of their relationship with other reps. This can be a great source of information for more than the products they represent.

To make an appointment with a rep from a company, simply contact the company that you are interested in, and ask for customer service. They will be able to tell you who services your area and put you in contact with your rep. Usually, the rep will meet with you in your office. You are on your way to developing a useful relationship for your practice.

Conducting Office Meetings

Because the use of time is critical for the entire eyecare team, the best office managers have learned how to make staff meetings productive. Staff meetings can be an excellent way of improving office productivity and morale, provided certain guidelines are followed.

Meeting Schedule

One of the most important items for the successful eyecare team is an ongoing meeting schedule. This schedule allows the team to know that there is time set aside for them because during most busy days there is little time to answer questions, speak about philosophy, or discuss suggestions. A regularly followed meeting schedule can accomplish this, but the schedule should be written out in advance and publicly displayed so that there can be no excuse for forgetting.

A full staff meeting should be held at least once a year to give the physician or office administrator a chance to fill everyone in on annual goals and the practice's general progress. With large organizations, the annual meeting also serves to establish camaraderie between employees who otherwise rarely meet.

In addition to this large meeting, smaller meetings should be held on a daily, weekly, and monthly basis. For example, mini-meetings involving only the key office figures (ie, the eyecare professional and office supervisors) can be very effective. These meetings can be about 5 minutes long and should occur at the start of each day so that the office schedule can be discussed and any potential problems can be avoided.

For organizations with fewer than 15 employees, a weekly and monthly full staff meeting should also be held. If there are 15 or more employees, a weekly meeting of only department heads would be more productive.

Successful meetings begin with setting time frames. To be effective a meeting must have a beginning and an ending time. If a meeting is too long, the staff is punished. Direction and effectiveness may be lost.

Once a time for the staff meeting is established, employees should be notified in advance. Surprise meetings are much less effective than planned ones. Also, the most effective meetings start on time regardless of who is there. (The most powerful reminder of the importance of being on time that you can receive is seeing that a meeting has begun without you!)

It is also vital to hold meetings during normal working hours. When employees are asked to come in early or stay late, they are being punished. They may also be preoccupied with other things at the beginning or end of the day. Instead, a meeting should be planned for a certain time, such as 3 to 5 PM, and no patient appointments should be scheduled during that time slot.

Meeting Agenda

The more attendees that know in advance about a proposed meeting, the more smoothly and efficiently it will proceed. Distribute a written agenda ahead of time, even if the gathering concerns only one matter. Announcing meeting topics in advance allows employees to prepare for the topics of discussion, and reassures them that they need not worry about the proceedings at hand. (It also prevents them from wasting precious hours doing so.) The staff should also have the opportunity to add their concerns. This accomplishes two things: 1) it lets the eyecare team know that they have input into how things may occur, and 2) it demonstrates that the physician/manager is organized and cares about the quality of service he or she is giving.

The agenda should begin with a discussion of the progress made on points brought up at the previous meeting, a discussion of new developments, and a problem-solving session.

When problem-solving, there are several techniques to remember if you hope to avoid a pointless complaint session. First, only invite problems that have a solution. Employees can be told, for example, that they may only bring up a problem if they have a potential solution for it. Next, encourage a positive atmosphere. Asking each attendee what good things have happened in the office that week is an effective mood-setting meeting technique. At first the staff may draw a blank, but eventually they'll come up with answers that help give the meeting an up-beat tone.

Remember, it is imperative that every employee be asked to voice an opinion on every problem that is brought up.

Final Notes

Comfortable gatherings often run unnecessarily long, so never offer too many amenities during the meetings themselves. Some of the most efficient short meetings are best held with attendees standing up, rather than sitting down in soft chairs. Do not waste time with coffee or cigarettes, especially during longer meetings held to review valuable business proposals. Such amenities only provide expensive distractions, especially when they spill or burn holes in important papers.

Employee surveys have indicated that 75% of all staff meetings are thought to be a waste of time. This is a grim statistic to battle against, but by following the techniques outlined above, staff meetings can be an enjoyable and productive experience for both management and employees.

Office Policy Manual

The rules for employment should ideally be expressed in a comprehensive office policy manual covering the following areas:

Introduction
General policies
    Accidents
    Bonding
    Common sense
    Compensation
    Confidential information
    Continuing education
    Employee status
    Employer/employee conferences
    General conduct
    General duties
    Grievances
    Hours
    Insurance
    Leave of absence (medical)
    Malpractice insurance
    Maternity
    New employees
    Overtime
    Paid holidays
    Payday
    Personal appearance
    Personal time off
    Personnel records
    Phone calls
    Policy review
    Professional courtesy
    Resignation
    Robbery
    Salary
    Sick leave
    Smoking
    Staff lounge
    Standards of conduct
    Tardiness
    Termination
    Time off policies
    Work hours
Conclusion
Acknowledgment (employee)
Policy against harassment
Acknowledgment (doctor)
Waiver of life insurance, dental insurance, and health insurance benefits

Examples and outlines of office policy manuals are available through professional organizations such as the American Optometric Association and the American Academy of Ophthalmology. They are available through bookstores and stationery suppliers, as well.

Staff Job Descriptions

Every single staff member of the eyecare team has two inalienable rights. The first is to know exactly what it is they are expected to do. The second is to be told how they are doing at it. This means that, along with the rules of employment (office policy manual), there must also exist two other components: protocols for job performance, and job evaluations. (We'll look at staff evaluation later in this chapter.)

Job descriptions describe the staff member's responsibility. Protocols describe how to do the job. When both job descriptions and protocols exist, practices can create cross training and never be at a loss under an emergency situation where only one person in the organization knows how to perform the job.

Ophthalmic Technician

Position Objective

To perform an extensive number of data collection functions as delegated by the physician to allow for proper professional diagnosis of patients' conditions and to do so in a way that instills patient confidence in the treatment.

Primary Responsibilities

Triage

1. Determining which patient should be taken next from the waiting room to have treatment initiated.
2. Escort all patients from the waiting room to the data collection or other appropriate room.
3. Following work-up, see that patients are escorted to the next appropriate examination room, advised as to who will see them next, and made comfortable during their wait.
4. Maintain a smooth flow of patients to the physician, altering the test sequence as required.
5. Determine which patient the physician will see next.

Communication

6. Acquaint all new patients with the office procedures they will experience.
7. Inform patients of the purpose of all tests personally performed and how they will be affected during the tests.
8. Put patients more at ease by informing them of the anticipated waiting time before they will be treated by the physician.
9. Confirm patient adherence to all contact lens procedures.
10. When appropriate, instruct patients in contact lens handling and care procedures.

Patient Care

11. History taking: Obtain a history including the chief complaint, history of present illness, past history (ocular and general), family history (ocular and general), and history of allergies and medications (ocular and general).

12. Measurements: Perform documentation and measurement tasks including measuring and recording the following:
    a. Visual acuity, both distance and near, and with and without spectacles.
    b. Amplitude of accommodation and range of accommodation including near-point of accommodation, both with and without spectacles.
    c. Preliminary optical measurements leading to the determination of the patient's refractive error by the ophthalmologist.
    d. Spectacle data, including sphere, cylinder, and axis by lensometry; whether it is single vision, bifocal or trifocal; whether they are glass or plastic lenses; and the wearing habits for each pair used.
    e. Muscle balance, to include the horizontal and vertical deviations by the Maddox rod or equivalent test, and the near point of convergence.
    f. Intraocular pressure (tonometry).
    g. Aqueous humor outflow (tonography).
    h. Central field of vision by tangent screen and the peripheral field of vision by perimeter (perimetry).
    i. Corneal curvature (keratometry) and vertical width of the palpebral fissure.
    j. Interpupillary distance for distance and near.
    k. Practical microbiology including the preparation of smears and scrapings of the ocular adnexa. Taking specimens for culture including handling microbiological instruments and media, and the proper recording of patient data.
    l. Comprehensive ocular motility measurements including:
        1. Measuring horizontal and vertical deviations using both the Maddox rod (or equivalent test), prism, and cover test.
        2. Determining whether a deviation is a phoria or a tropia, using the cover/uncover, cover/cover, and alternate cover tests.
        3. Measuring the presence, absence, or degree of fusion.
        4. Measuring the presence, absence, or degree of stereopsis.
        5. Measuring the muscle fields using the Lancaster, Hess-Lees Screen, or similar tests.
    m. Exophthalmometry quantitating the amount of ocular prominence.
    n. Schirmer test or similar procedure quantitating the amount of tear production.
    o. External ophthalmic photography and fundus photography.

13. Clinical assisting: Assist the ophthalmologist in the performance of complex clinical procedures such as fluorescein fundus photography, contact lens fitting, gonioscopy, ophthalmodynamometry, irrigating of the lacrimal system, and other tasks requiring special assistance.

14. Surgical assisting: Provide limited assistance to the ophthalmologist in performing surgical operations and keep surgical instruments sterile and ready for use.

15. For contact lens patients, clean and polish lenses as appropriate.

16. Make certain that all preschool children are tested for visual anomalies.

17. Assist the front office personnel in answering the phone or giving attention to immediate patient problems.
18. Direct care:
    a. Change eye dressings.
    b. Instill eye drops such as topical anesthetics, mydriatics, and cycloplegics.
    c. Instill eye ointments of various types.
    d. Administer oral medications in tablet, capsule, or liquid form.
    e. Administer other medications as directed.
    f. Transmit instruction in home care.

Administrative

19. Ophthalmic instruments and spectacles: Maintain and adjust ophthalmic instruments at the user level, to include the following:
    a. Keep exposed lenses, mirrors, and prisms clean.
    b. Replace burned out bulbs.
    c. Keep chin rest and head rest papers fresh.
    d. Make internal adjustments in focus and optical alignment and calibrate such instruments as tonometers, slit lamps, and keratometers.

Effective Authority

20. Determine which station and which staff member should treat patients.
21. Instill dilating drops when appropriate for indirect or cycloplegic examination.
22. Perform whatever screening tests are deemed appropriate in addition to the minimum requirements.
23. Select which patient should be seen next from the waiting room and by the physician.
24. Eliminate ancillary screening tests or seek assistance to perform them when time constraints are affecting patient flow.

Hiring Staff

Once management understands what it is they wish employees to do (job descriptions), and the rules of the working environment (office policy manual) have been established, the next step is to identify and interview the appropriate personnel. Every practice wants to have a dynamic, exciting, and people-loving staff who are superbly trained and understand both the professional and the service side of eyecare.

The Office Manager as Casting Director

On Interstate 4, southwest of Orlando, FL, a striking gold and purple building fronts the freeway. A big sign defines the company's mission in one eloquent simple word, *casting*. It's the Walt Disney World personnel office where that one word says a lot, not just about Disney, but all companies that are focused on service. They don't just hire people for jobs. Rather, they "cast performers for a role." In service-focused companies, such as eyecare, patient service jobs are thought of as less like factory work and much more like theater. At a play, the audience files in, the curtain goes up, and the actors make their entrances and speak their lines. If each and every cast member (not to mention the writer, director, stage hands, costumers, make-up artists, and lighting technicians) has prepared himself or herself and their theater well, the audience enjoys the show and tells others about it.

In today's service driven business world, you, as the office manager, are more director than boss, more choreographer than administrator. Your front line people are the actors, and your customers are the audience for whom they must perform. Everyone else is a support group, charged with making sure that the theater is right, the sets are ready, and the actors are primed and prepared.

The independent eyecare practitioner manager has to prepare the cast, know their cues, and hit the mark by delivering their lines and improvising when the other cast members (or someone in the audience) disrupt the carefully plotted flow of performance. And, once the curtain goes up, all you can do is watch and whisper from the wings. You are not allowed on stage because you would simply get in the way. Most independent eyecare offices spend too little time finding the right people as prospects for their cast. Here is an example of what the most successful service businesses have done:

For the grand opening of the Grand Hyatt Wailea, one of the crown jewel Hawaiian resorts, 6,000 people were screened to fill 1,200 jobs.

When Nordstrom opened its east coast store in Tyson Corner, Virginia, it interviewed 3,000 people to fill 400 front line jobs.

Applicants for positions with the St. Petersburg based Florida Power Corporation attend job preview days where experienced performers demonstrate everything from rolling cable to answering the telephone. The realistic view of the company's work helps people select the positions they are best able to fill and deselect themselves from areas where they clearly won't fit.

The key to a successful and dynamic staff is to hire as if you were casting.

Finding Employee Candidates

Typically, the best methods for finding employee candidates is through personnel advertisement and networking. Newspaper or journal ads take longer because there is a waiting period until a particular ad may appear. Simply asking around can be very effective. Let ophthalmic product representatives and even your patients know that you need to fill a certain position. Lastly, one can sometimes identify personnel by calling a colleague's office and asking if they have recently interviewed anyone whom they did not choose and would they mind sharing the résumé with you.

Hiring winners is an art rather than a talent. What should you do to hire a winner? For starters, you may want to go searching at a local fast-food restaurant. If I were to tell you that the ideal person to hire for your practice may be working at a fast-food restaurant, you might give me a double take. Yet it's true.

Winning employees are likely to work in busy, high-traffic service environments such as fast-food restaurants, banks, and supermarkets. The employee who remains cool under the pressure of public demand is the one you want.

You are well aware of the pressures you face each day. You certainly don't need the added pressure of hiring a person and then finding out that he or she is wrong for the job, or that the job is wrong for that person. The end result—firing the employee or having him or her resign—brings you back to square one, and probably more frustrated than ever.

How do you avoid this trap? How do you hire a winner the first time around? The secret is to find people who are able to do their jobs with enthusiasm and who truly care about the work they do.

If the employee cares about getting lunch-hour customers through a fast-food line quickly and error-free—and he or she does it with a smile—chances are that person will have the same conviction and enthusiasm for any job.

Such people are quick to smile, warm, articulate, and well-groomed. Typically, they enjoy interaction with other people and are able to have fun regardless of the pressures or demands. They have an internal self-motivating character, so they are quick and eager to learn. Don't be discouraged, however, if you are not successful at first; keep searching until you find someone you feel is worth talking to.

Once you come across that person, try striking up a conversation this way: "I couldn't help but notice how well you do your job. It looks like you really enjoy it." After the person smiles and thanks you, follow with this: "Have you ever thought about a career in health care?" At that point, give the person a business card and an invitation to discuss employment opportunities.

Effective Ads

An effective ad is one in which the job position is accurately described. This can prevent misunderstandings and possible future litigation. For example, consider the following ad:

"Help Wanted: Experienced ophthalmic assistant/technologist for busy eyecare office. Must be proficient in lensometry and perimetry."

If a candidate who possesses these skills is ultimately hired and later asked to perform chores other than perimetry and lensometry such as assisting in the maintenance of the exam lanes, contact lenses, etc., there may be resentment. Such resentment then begins the employer/employee relationship on poor footing. Compare the previous advertisement with the following:

"Help Wanted: Experienced ophthalmic assistant/technologist for busy eyecare office. Duties include lensometry and perimetry."

This advertisement is more open in that it uses the word "include." This allows the prospective employee to ask questions relative to the job specifics and it also protects the employer from false or misleading advertising.

Because eyecare professionals live in an increasingly litigious world, care must also be taken to avoid discriminatory advertising. Actually, eyecare professionals would prefer stable, young, attractive men and women who are dynamic and bright. Yet, laws exist that protect prospective employees from discrimination. Specifically, one of these laws states that ophthalmic personnel may not be discriminated against with regard to age, race, or religion. If the following advertisement appeared:

"Tall female, attractive ophthalmic assistant, between the ages of 19 and 25 . . ."

A short, chunky, 21-year-old who possessed the right skills might find an attorney to claim that the reason he wasn't chosen was due to discrimination.

Legal Discrimination

Discrimination may be said to be legal if it is a standard for employment. For example, some military and airlines have a standard for all employees in that they have a certain height or age requirement. Thus, if the eyecare professional has a standard for employees who are female, attractive, and between the ages of 19 and 25, then such a position may be legal. Prudence dictates, however, that because each eyecare practice may be different, a labor attorney should be consulted to rule on legal discrimination prior to placing such an advertisement.

Narrowing the Field

After receiving the first résumés, the next step in narrowing the field is to contact the candidate by phone. This is particularly important because it can reveal other characteristics that cannot be communicated in writing. These characteristics include, but are not limited to:

1. Voice friendliness
2. Attitude
3. Articulateness
4. Intelligence

From a legal standpoint, it is important to avoid choosing any candidate because of discrimination. Therefore, when making initial telephone contact, keep all notes you may take in a separate personal file.

Conducting the Interview

Once the eyecare professional has advertised and chosen several candidates, the interview phase of hiring can begin. As with advertisements, federal laws exist that protect prospective employees from being discriminated against. According to these laws, age, race, religion, and certain handicaps may not prevent the prospective employee from becoming a candidate provided that the person has the skills required. However, the eyecare professional has the right to choose between candidates. If two different candidates seem to have equal skills, the eyecare professional may select one of his or her choice. However, if the candidate who is not chosen challenges the decision, the employer should be able to prove that the decision was based on factors other than discrimination.

Questions, Questions

In order to avoid an untoward situation, the eyecare professional should be careful to interview for the job only! A rejected applicant for ophthalmic employment may be considered to have been discriminated against, if asked about subjects unrelated to the job itself. For example, questions about family or outside interests are considered to be job unrelated. The fact that a prospective employee has 10 children and has been married 11 times doesn't have anything to do with the ability to perform the job. Therefore, asking questions about family is irrelevant. On the other hand, an employer may inquire about the candidate's record regarding attendance and punctuality.

The interviewer, whether physician or administrator, must also be cautious regarding exactly how questions are asked. Consider this interview dialogue:

Employer: "Where do you live?"

Employee: "Why do you ask?"

Employer: "Well, I want to make sure that you can get here on time, regularly."

This line of questioning can be considered to be discriminatory. If the candidate wasn't chosen, then he/she could sue the employer and say, "I *can* get there on time. Just because I live 200 miles away shouldn't have anything to do with it!" This candidate is absolutely correct. An employer may not consider distance as a criteria. Here is how the conversation could have been handled:

Employer: "How would you rate your attendance record?"

Employee: "Good."

Employer: "I put great importance on consistent punctuality. Is there any reason you feel that you could not meet my expectations?"

For more help on interview questions, see Form 8, Interview Response Chart, in the Appendix. As the interview proceeds, the eyecare professional can also use an interview response chart to help remember some important points of the interview. As the interviewer would likely talk to multiple candidates for a single position, using an interview response chart will help one remember the individual candidates and their specific characteristics.

Keep in mind that throughout the interview you must evaluate certain traits that spell either success or failure. Identifying a potential employee who is doomed to failure before it is too late can save a lot of time and money. The best way to do this is to identify traits of employees who have already failed. Make sure not to hire anyone who exhibits such traits. (This rule of thumb also holds true when determining whether or not current employees should be promoted.)

Sometimes observation of nonverbal communication can tell more than speaking. Here are some guidelines on observing body language:

1. Crossed arms or feet generally indicate an attitude of closure, signifying an unwillingness to listen.
2. Leaning forward indicates a desire to communicate better and an interest in listening.
3. Fidgeting indicates nervousness and self-consciousness.
4. Making eye contact indicates the ability to communicate and connect.

Straight Talk

During the interview, provide a clear job description and discuss responsibilities thoroughly. Few things are more disconcerting than having the employee find out after the fact that job responsibilities are not what he or she had been expecting.

Conversely, when a new employee discovers that the job is just as it was described, he or she is more likely to fall in love with it. Such bonding and feeling of belonging and enjoyment create the magic glue that keeps employees satisfied and on the job long-term.

Next in the interview process, let the prospective employee know how you grade success and where the opportunities for growth exist. People who are allowed to write their own job contracts seem to do best on the job. Lastly, have a frank discussion about compensation, and make sure it is clearly understood by the interviewee.

Many practices find that issuing a pre-employment test is helpful. These tests do not always carry the greatest validity, but they serve as good indicators. Established tests that you may want to consider using include:

1. The EEF Wonderlic Personnel Test, by Wonderlic and Associates, Northfield, IL.
2. The Cardall Test of Practical Judgment, by Alfred J. Cardall, Princeton, NJ.
3. Standard word processing or typing tests.

It is difficult to assess specific skills from observing one particular demonstration such as performing a refraction, scheduling a patient, etc. One excellent way of handling this is to simply invite the prospective employee (on a paid basis) to spend a few days in the office. This is beneficial for both parties. Make it clear that this is a no-obligation offer.

In summary, a carefully constructed interview, plus the use of an interview response chart, can aid the eyecare professional interviewer in tracking the important data regarding a candidate. After all interviews have concluded, the hiring team can carefully compare both the responses and comments with the interview response charts, thus ensuring a successful way to decide between candidates.

Staff Orientation

Once you hire someone, conduct a job orientation that is useful for both you and the new employee. This is an excellent time to distribute the protocol of how a job is actually done. Don't take this step lightly, because it is at this crucial point where both of you can decide whether the relationship is worth continuing.

To take full advantage of the orientation process, it is important to understand the difference between teachable and unteachable skills. Don't waste your time trying to teach skills such as initiative, ability to learn, resilience, flexibility, and common sense. If the employees do not come ready with these skills, odds are against their succeeding. Teachable skills include how to handle directions, how to plan, how to ask questions, how to manage, and how to delegate responsibility.

Here is a summary of orientation steps:

1. Make sure the orientation period is clearly defined, and set a clear agenda. Distribute copies of the agenda to the appropriate staff.
2. Each day ask the employee what he or she has learned and provide the worker with an opportunity to ask questions.
3. Provide frequent feedback to the employee on progress made.

In order to create a productive training schedule, it is important to first outline all the tasks necessary. Second, prioritize these tasks into the following categories: most important, important, and least important. Once the prioritization has taken place, divide all of the individual elements into the period of time allowed for the training session. (eg, 30, 60, and 90 days.) Here is an example:

Technician Training Schedule

1. Acquaint yourself with our charting system and history-taking methods.
   A. Charting categories include new patient, established patient, follow-up, glaucoma check, postoperative visit, visual fields, laser, emergency (short and long), preoperative visit, (subjective, objective, assessment, and plans [SOAP]), etc.
      Know the location of the patient's history, ocular testing, and doctor notes.
   B. When taking histories know the chief complaint number one, with the disease-related complaint, and also if the chief complaint is not disease-related.
      Always ask the patient if there has been a vision change, discomfort, or if he or she is taking any eye medications.
      Frequently ask the patient if he or she is taking systemic medications, or is experiencing changes, allergies, or diseases.
2. Know the equipment
   A. In the start-up room, know the lens analyzer, auto-refractor, and auto-keratometer.
   B. Check the visual field analyzer, and know the Vistech glare test.
   C. In the exam room check the projectors first (two types), slit lamp use and prep-cleaning, the pinhole, the penlight, the chair controls, the light panel, and the light system outside rooms.
3. Follow a tech and observe patient work-up.
   A. Know the history of the patient's complaints and the length of time since their last visit. Pursuing complaints appropriately means asking questions as to the date of onset, severity, duration, and frequency of the chief complaint. Take visual acuities, with or without the patient's glasses, as well as distance, near, or intermediate measurements.
   B. Summarizing, abbreviations, location of drops, number one complaint must be disease-related regarding Medicare guidelines.
   C. The trainee may chart and begin performing startup testing, and later take histories and acuities under observation.
4. The trainee can chart motility and gross visual fields.
5. The trainee can take histories and acuities of very routine visits.

6. The trainee must learn external ocular tests such as pupils, extraocular movements, muscle balance, and gross visual fields, and learn when to pinhole vision.
7. The trainee must learn to administer eye drops and learn the patch technique.
8. The trainee must learn scribing and superbill.
9. The trainee must learn auxiliary tests such as the Amsler grid, over-refracting, laser assisting, office surgery setup, autoclaving, office drops and samples, manual potential acuity meter, Maddox rod, etc.
10. The trainee must learn refractometry:
    A. Begin with the meaning of lens analysis and autorefraction comparison, the meaning of visual acuity changes especially as they pertain to cataracts and age-related macular degeneration. Know the setup of the phoropter for the patient and for lenses.
    B. Know the patient's visual complaints as related to refraction.
    C. Measure the first refractions 1 week after cataract surgery.
    D. Know automated refraction versus the phoropter.

It is helpful to both trainer and trainee if you develop skill objectives for each task to be learned. Well-written objectives contain behaviors that are measurable. Words that indicate a measurable or observable skill include demonstrate, list, identify, perform, explain, describe, recognize, and measure. Words that are not measurable include learn, understand, comprehend, and discern.

Suppose you wanted to train an employee to irrigate the eye. A set of objectives for that skill could be:

1. Identify the indications for irrigation.
2. Select the appropriate irrigating solution.
3. Demonstrate the proper irrigating technique, providing for run-off.
4. Explain the importance of irrigating for an adequate amount of time.

An excellent way to determine how a new staff member is progressing is to let your staff evaluate the new employee's performance. The front office team, the business office team, and the clinical office team are frequently in the best position to see how the orientation period is going. If invited to evaluate, their comments can be quite insightful. In fact, your staff can often tell you within days whether or not a new employee is a winner.

Frequently, winners are made, not found. It's true that you can find a winner in a high-traffic service setting. Still, they may be rough around the edges and will need to be cultivated. A big reason that employees fail is because they are not adequately coached.

Effective Supervision

Success

The results of a recent survey evaluating those elements that made for success in the eyecare professional's office revealed three major areas. First, in every single instance where success occurred it was because the employee had possessed the raw skills with which to succeed. This was not to say that they possessed all the skills, but at least the basics needed to succeed in an eyecare office were present.

The second reason that success occurred was that during the initial interview, the expectations of the employee were met. This included an accurate job description, job performance evaluation, and growth potential.

A third reason that success continues is because an employee realizes that although his or her compensation and benefits are paid by the eyecare professional, he or she is really working for himself or herself. This means that employees who take total responsibility for what happens can help manage and grow within the eyecare practice.

Another factor regarding success occurs when the following elements are present: knowledge of what tasks and jobs are to be accomplished, the action taken toward the accomplishments, and the reasonable time it takes to accomplish them. These three elements combined can make true success.

The last major area for successful inter-relationships between the eyecare professional and the employee is evidenced as follows:

1. Both employee and supervisor (eyecare professional) know the major mission, goal and/or objective of the practice.
2. Both parties know and understand the products and services to be extended.
3. Everyone (employer, supervisor, employee) realizes that they are in a sales situation where the product is superior health care to be delivered with the least anxiety and the greatest personal attention possible. This includes the sale of the employees themselves as an integral part of the health care team.
4. An understanding of exactly who the patient (customer) really is.
5. Understanding the psychological makeup of a patient, as well as fellow workers.
6. Nature has a way of producing what is expected versus what is merely wanted or hoped for. This proves that one really becomes what one thinks about most of the time. Positive expectations beget positive results.
7. Self-responsibility. (If it is to be, it is up to me.)
8. An understanding and appreciation of the 80/20 rule. (80% of all productivity is accomplished by 20% of the people.)
9. Personal growth is dictated by an internal thermostat, which may be reset.
10. Change can be implemented by understanding the desire (which must be strong, real, and visual), focused thinking about the desire in minute detail, and creating a route to follow as a path toward reaching the desired objective.
11. Practice does not make perfect, practice makes permanent. Only perfect practice makes perfect.
12. All feelings are controlled by thoughts. The daily stresses of employment in an eyecare office can be overcome through positive thinking.
13. Ninety-two percent of all worry is a waste of time.
14. "The raise will become effective as soon as you do."
15. The most important person in the office is the *patient*.
16. Mondays, traffic, and lunch hours don't care.
17. "There is no way to happiness. Happiness is the way." (Quote by Wayne Dyer from *Transformations* published by Nightingale - Conant Inc. in 1990.)

In addition to the above-mentioned criteria for success is the understanding that the key in all organizations is people who are motivated to care, perform, and foster the missions and goals of the eyecare practice. Success is not a destination. Success is a process.

Inspection

A job description, however, is only as good as the person who oversees it. An employee will discharge his or her assigned duties more efficiently when the supervisor assumes the responsibility of inspecting these duties. One appropriate adage in management is: If one expects, one must inspect. A close working relationship between the office manager, supervisor, and physician, with frequent feedback in communication, can improve any eyecare practice.

Another key to good management is taken from Tom Peters' book *In Search of Excellence* published by Balatine in 1994. In this magnificent book on how the best-run corporations handle personnel, the term Management By Walking Around (MBWA) is introduced. MBWA simply means that the supervisor walks around looking at how systems are working. It means stopping periodically anywhere from the reception desk, to the insurance department, to his or her own office. MBWA enforces the image that the eyecare professional is truly interested in all details of how the office is running. The highest achievers in eyecare practice keep a high level of team spirit by occasionally appearing, making eye contact, and briefly discoursing with the employee team.

Yet another skill for keeping the team together and developing a level of excellence and excitement is to develop the habit of catching team members doing something correctly. Too often team members hear from the doctor only when they do something wrong. Catching somebody doing something correctly simply means to watch them do something right and tell them how much they are appreciated when they do. There is no way to calculate the amount of good that is generated with such action.

A recent article, cited in *On Errors In Surveys* by Irvington Press, 1993, by practice management guru W. Edwards Deming, demonstrates how a poorly managed system, not the workers, leads to defects and poor quality management. This is excerpted from one of Deming's famous seminars entitled "Red Bead Experiment." Ten seminar attendees are chosen and assigned jobs by Deming. Six are what he calls "willing workers," two are inspectors, one is a chief inspector, and one is a recorder. Deming explains that the company has received orders to make white beads. Unfortunately, the raw materials used in production contain a certain number of defects or "red beads." Both the white beads and the red beads are in a plastic container. The six willing workers are given a paddle with 20 indentations in it and told to dip it into the container, shake it, and pull it out with each indentation filled with a bead. Then they are instructed to take the paddle to the first inspector who, in turn, counts the red beads or "defects." The second inspector does the same, and the chief inspector checks their tally, which the recorder then dutifully records.

One worker happens to draw out a paddle with 15 white beads and five red beads and thus gets a merit raise. One worker has six white beads and 14 red beads and is put on probation. In the next round, the worker who had 14 red beads now has only eight red beads and the worker with only five red beads now has 10 red beads. Deming, playing the role of the misguided manager, thinks he understands what's happening. The worker who got the merit raise is getting sloppy, the raise must have gone to his head. Meanwhile, the worker on probation had been frightened into performing better. And so it continues, a cycle of reward and punishment while management fails to understand that the defects are built into the system and that the workers have very little to do with it. The moral of the story is that the system is frequently at fault in failing to train, analyze, and measure appropriately.

Delegation

Every office manager must develop the highest possible degree of effective delegation in order to spur the growth of the practice's most valuable asset—its staff. As eyecare professionals continue to seek solutions to their economic viability, they look for as many appreciating assets as possible. No asset can be more appreciating than staff. Employees are far more valuable to any eyecare office than typewriters, computers, instrumentation, or office space. Yet the amount that staff members will appreciate is directly dependent on the way in which tasks are delegated to them.

It is management's job to create the maximum yield as a return on investment in staff. To this extent, the more the management can enrich the staff, the quicker the return on the investment becomes.

Delegation is the key developer of people. The first rule of delegation is to excise the following myths that prevent effective delegation:

1. The employee doesn't know enough or isn't competent enough. The only way to test the capability of staff is to give them more to do than they have ever done before, allowing them the latitude to make mistakes and learn.

2. If you want it done right, you have to do it yourself. Here the biggest failure in eyecare management is the inability to move from doing the job to managing the job. Because the natural tendency is to fall back on the comfort zone of doing it yourself rather than delegating, just being alert to this myth will help. Management's ultimate job regarding staff is to manage—to get other people to do certain tasks, not to operate the practice alone.

3. There is not enough time to delegate. The swamped supervisor says, "I don't have enough time to sit down and explain this to somebody else, I just have to get going with it." Failure to take the time to walk the employee through and to show how a specific job is to be done results in nondelegation and frustration. The point is that there is always enough time, and taking the time to delegate well is one of the most effective investments of time.

4. Because you are good at it, you should do it. Spending time on tasks that have already become routine is wasteful. The key here is that whatever the supervisor has mastered (ie, what has become simple to do should be delegated.)

5. People will think you are not doing your best if you get somebody else to do it. Often the executive staff believes that they can only be perceived as doing well if everybody knows that they are on top of everything and they know what is going on all the time. In today's complex eyecare practice, one can never know what is going on all the time. But with the proper system, the good manager can know by accessing the people who do know. Henry Ford was once challenged that he didn't know the details about how cars were made. Ford responded, "Yes I realize what I don't know. But I can get any answer you wish by merely picking up this telephone." The secret here is one does not have to be able to perform the task in order to manage it.

This brings us to the following six basic principles of effective delegation:

1. Delegate the entire job. When a staff member knows he or she is in charge of the total task from beginning to end, they become highly motivated. Every single person on staff should have at least one job for which they are totally responsible.

2. To build competence, delegate gradually. Assign an entire smaller task and then work up to tougher, longer ones.

3. Match the skills of the job to the person. Delegating a task that is too easy for the person is just as poor as delegating a job that is so difficult that he or she doesn't have a high chance of succeeding.

4. Delegate with participation and the opportunity for discussion. There is a direct relationship between the amount of time an employee spends discussing the job and the

---

Table 5-1.

Common Employee Failure Traits

1. Lack of respect for other people's time.
2. Lack of concern for personal appearance.
3. Arrogance.
4. Habitual excuse-making with minimal output.
5. The "pay me first and I'll produce later" attitude.
6. The belief that advancement is an entitlement.
7. Reluctance to help coworkers and reluctance to volunteer for special assignments.
8. Constant complaining.
9. Refusal to accept responsibility.

---

employee's commitment to doing it correctly. When effectively performed, this creates "job ownership."

5. Delegate for specific results. The manager/supervisor who helps employees keep their eye on the ball and keeps them looking at the results also helps the employees continue to think of the results they have been hired to accomplish.

6. Leave the delegatee alone. Once you have delegated the job, delegate all of it and don't take it back. Supervisors take the job back by continually checking on the person, continually asking for feedback, and then making comments and trying to make changes along the way.

By first eradicating the myths of delegation and replacing them with six effective principles of delegation, the office manager can begin to exercise greater control over the practice's most appreciating asset—the staff.

Employee Evaluations

Staff evaluations are most effective when they are performed on a predetermined basis. The function of job appraisal versus salary appraisal is best handled at 6-month intervals. For example: The employee is evaluated for how the job is being performed and given 6 months to either meet, maintain, or exceed a given standard. In this manner, salary appraisal can take place in a positive environment.

The training and learning cycles of individuals vary according to their education and experience in life. However, certain principles are universal. They are as follows:

1. Behavior that's rewarded persists.
2. Every staff member wants to be appreciated and have the opportunity to learn and grow.
3. Measure performance frequently and include feedback.

Good management understands both success and failure traits. If one understands why most employees fail, he or she can take steps to help them succeed or to avoid choosing failure in the first place. Table 5-1 shows nine common employee failure traits.

In order to provide specific issues for evaluation and to ensure that evaluations are uniform, an employee appraisal form may be used (Form 9, Appendix). This also provides continuity for the employee, who then knows what to expect at evaluation time.

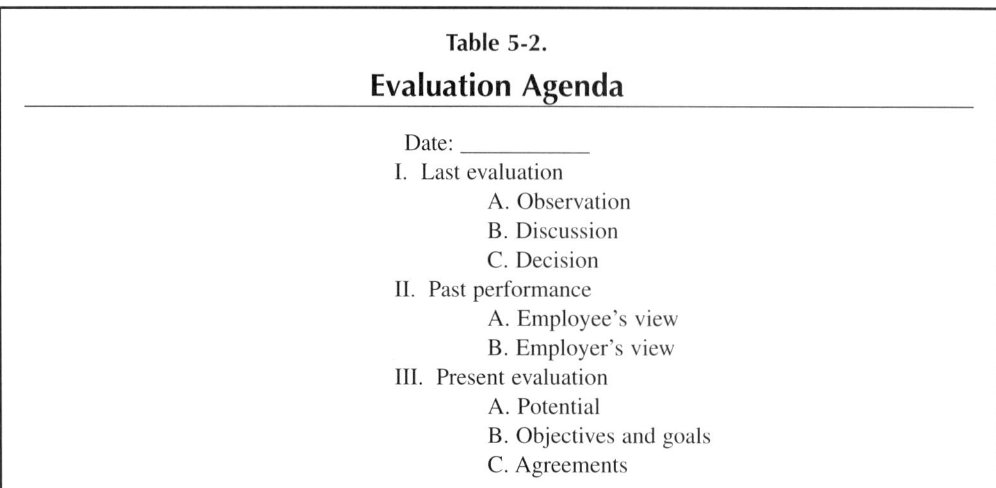

Table 5-2.
Evaluation Agenda

Date: ___________
I. Last evaluation
      A. Observation
      B. Discussion
      C. Decision
II. Past performance
      A. Employee's view
      B. Employer's view
III. Present evaluation
      A. Potential
      B. Objectives and goals
      C. Agreements

Because employee appraisals are time consuming and demanding, management can keep track of what has happened in the past through the use of an evaluation agenda. This agenda summarizes what has occurred in the past and addresses present and future issues as well (Table 5-2).

Using a written evaluation agenda allows the manager or supervisor to make appropriate notes a permanent part of the employee's file. This can be an invaluable tool in the case of dissatisfaction on either part, and will serve as an excellent document in the case of litigation.

Discipline

Perhaps the greatest challenges an office manager faces first are accurately measuring employee performance, and second, counseling to improve it. Standards of acceptable behavior must be carefully weighed against a number of considerations. However, once it's determined that there is a problem, the solution depends mainly on a reasonable and systematic disciplinary procedure.

Every good manager recognizes the value of discretion and does not make occasional minor policy infringements a part of the permanent record. Extenuating circumstances must always be considered. Infrequent lateness, for example, may be excused or even overlooked. However, if tardiness occurs several times in a month, an official warning would not be out of place before such behavior becomes habitual.

Supervisory reprimands must be based on a combination of factors that usually include the employee's approach to work and the nature of his or her responsibilities. It's always important to weigh the magnitude of the infraction against the employee's overall performance record, as well as the employer's expectations for performance. Whatever the standards, however, undesirable behavior must be brought to the employee's attention immediately. Whenever possible, those judgment calls should appear as clear and as unwavering as those of a baseball umpire.

Having a system that documents performance problems in a timely manner, reinforced by written records that track employee progress or lack thereof, gives personnel a clear message of employer expectations. A company's intent is especially clear when it distributes an employee manual for training and future reference. In such cases, the first instance of verbal and/or written counseling is actually a second communication from management that simply confirms the employee manual's message.

Recently I discovered a five-step form which is ideal for communicating and recording disciplinary issues with employees. Each sheet is color-coded, self-carbonized, and a bit longer than the preceding sheet. It enables both the employee and the employer to receive a complete history of all previous notices and discussions on the matter on one sheet of paper, with no photocopies to make or lose. (You can obtain a free sample of this progressive discipline form from the manufacturer, Henion Business Forms in Madera, CA, by telephoning 1-800-859-7150.)

If you use this form, or one like it, as part of your progressive discipline program, show it to every new employee and explain that it presents an opportunity to correct undesirable behavior. Post a blank form on the bulletin board explaining that the form is an early warning about problems before they become major issues, and indicate that a change in job performance is needed. Explain also that the form will become part of the employee's personnel file.

This type of form, backed with these procedures, demonstrates that you mean business and may serve to weaken intentions of misbehavior. In addition, the form documents your efforts as an employer to work with employees to bring their performance up to standard.

Using this form, successive comments and warnings are obvious at a glance. By the time you reach step five, no misplaced documentation or misunderstandings are possible; a situation that is particularly desirable if termination should become necessary.

When recording an employee warning, be certain to allow a reasonable length of time before a follow-up review is made (at least 30 days) to determine whether there has been improvement or whether additional corrective action is necessary (Form 10, Appendix). The warning should be given in a friendly but firm manner without any editorializing. Simply put, say it and shut up. This is one reason that management is considered more of an art than a science.

To protect against future disagreements about the nature or timing of the warning, employees should sign the form each time any entry is made. They should also receive a copy each time. However, supervisors should actively encourage discussion of the situation both at the time of the warning and later, if the employee requests it.

When you meet with employees to discuss performance issues, be sure to draft an agenda to ensure that you cover all necessary points. (Table 5-2 can be used for regular evaluations as well as problem sessions.) In addition, a formal plan can often be more convincing of the need for compliance than a casual, less-focused discussion of the problem. Make sure to leave plenty of time for the employee to register his or her own opinion of his or her progress and for the employee to document any relevant success or achievement.

Using an employee manual in conjunction with a progressive discipline form sends a message of consistency and fairness to employees. This, in turn, improves morale, productivity, and turnover rates.

If progressive discipline is handled properly, employees will never get to the point where you must simply terminate them. However, at times the act of termination is a responsibility of the supervisor or manager. The following guidelines will help you "lower the boom":

1. Hold the termination act in a private and secure place.
2. Have a third person present as a witness.
3. State what you are about to do.
4. Do not enter into a discussion. For example, "The purpose of this meeting is to advise you that effective immediately you are being terminated from your employment. This decision has been made and there is no discussion."
5. Delineate the terms of termination such as leave immediately, hand in your keys (uniform, books, etc.).

6. Hand the terminated employee a check for all services performed up to that date, including vacation time and any other benefits that are monetary in nature.
7. Be compassionate and understanding. Say, "I know this is a difficult thing for you and I am sorry I was the one who had to deliver the message."
8. Personally escort the terminated person out of the office.
9. Change the locks and distribute new keys to everyone.

Conclusion

The position of office manager has its responsibilities as well as its privileges. Certainly it is one of the most challenging positions in the practice. Not only is there the opportunity for personal growth, but the opportunity to help others grow as well. All this growth adds up to further the ongoing mission of medicine—better patient care.

Section II

CAREER MANAGEMENT

Résumés and Interviews

- The essential elements of identifying and hiring personnel are divided into the categories of résumés and interviews.

- Building a successful résumé is a springboard to hiring success.

- The key element in job search strategy is effective communication.

From time to time, every eyecare employee participates in the process of job attainment. In order to get the job of your dreams, you must communicate your talents and capabilities in a professional and organized manner.

Ideally, a prospective job should have a prepared job description detailing the elements of the expected areas of responsibility. In truth, most eyecare practices do not have this readily available. Prudence dictates that you be prepared even though you initially don't know exactly what is required. This can be identified later during the initial interview.

The Résumé

Professional search firms have documented the types of characteristics that comprise a successful résumé. Here are a few of the most often recommended guidelines:

1. Your résumé is essentially an ad. It is the most effective way of marketing and packaging yourself by describing information that supports your job objective as you see it. In order to attain a position, a competitive résumé should be a compilation of capabilities that will help you move into future employment (rather than merely a historical document).
2. A good résumé substantiates your positive qualities, skills, characteristics, and accomplishments. This will be the groundwork for building a prospective employer's confidence in you during contacts and interview meetings.
3. Understand that from the employer's perspective, there is only one question: "Why should I hire you?"
4. A résumé should contain all necessary facts about your background, abilities, and career track.
5. Your résumé should contain a brief list of your major accomplishments.
6. It should be concise and to the point.
7. It should include business and home addresses, zip codes, and telephone numbers of your current and former employers.
8. It should organize chronological data such as your work history and education, beginning with the most recent first.

The components of a résumé are (Form 13, Appendix):

1. Heading: Name, address, telephone number.
2. Summary: A short concise statement summarizing experiences, areas of expertise, qualifications, technical/professional skills, traits, and any other distinctions.
3. Objective: Identification of the area of the eyecare market that is being targeted for your future employment (front office, reception, technician, management, etc.).
4. Experience (employment history): List the most recent job and continue in reverse chronological order, including company name, years employed, and position(s). (Responsibility statement): A summary of selected items for each job description, including special assignments and general duties.
5. Certification (accomplishment statements): Statements that show your achievements and contributions to your previous organizations. Accomplishments generally should reflect a particular short-term project or specific application of a general responsibility.
6. Education: Summary of your educational background including highest degree, area of major, university, and location by city and state.

7. Activities (memberships): Memberships and offices held in relevant associations and organizations.
8. Other skills: List any other relevant skills you may have.

The following are additional guidelines for avoiding résumé pitfalls:

1. Don't use abbreviations.
2. Don't use odd size paper.
3. Don't put a snapshot or photo of yourself with your résumé unless it was specifically asked for.
4. Don't list references initially. Reserve them for the interview.
5. Don't include any personal data regarding age, marital status, number of children, or health.
6. Don't emphasize your educational background.
7. Don't leave any gaps between employment dates. List jobs by the year rather than the month and the year, but be certain to briefly state a good reason for any gap.

The Cover Letter

In addition to having a well-written résumé, good job candidates are recognized by their cover letters. An example to be used as a benchmark for cover letters is included in the appendix (Form 12).

The Interview

The key element in job search strategy is effective communication. The manner in which a candidate communicates significantly affects the impression left on others. It also determines success in obtaining interviews, meetings, and ultimately, job offers. It is important for the candidate to stimulate the other person's thinking or to clarify one's value with specific examples indicative of background, experience, and potential worth.

Active listening, supportive nonverbal communication, and persuasive verbal and written communications skills can enable a candidate to market himself or herself more effectively.

Listening alerts one to what is taking place and helps achieve the planned objectives in a meeting or interview. One can determine the assets and qualifications an employer values in a candidate by listening, as well as identifying job opportunities that might exist.

Body language can be interpreted both positively and negatively. It is very natural to be a little tense or nervous, but crossing your arms, clinching your fists, and drumming your fingers on a chair is a clear giveaway that you are uncomfortable. Such body language will certainly detract from the presentation because it conveys a lack of comfort and confidence. Instead, pretend that you are in an acting role: relax, smile, and be conscious of keeping your facial expressions tranquil. Sit up straight but not stiffly, and lean forward a little (this indicates interest and eagerness).

Good eye contact establishes rapport and shows that you are attentive and interested. If the interview is being conducted by more than one person, the key is to maintain eye contact with the group by slowly scanning each face as you are presenting.

Most interviewers will assume that you will never dress better on the job than how you are dressed for the job interview. The lesson here is to make certain that you are dressed according to the importance and formality of a potential position. Most of all, pay close attention to personal grooming.

The interview is not just a time for the potential employer to look you over, but also a time for you to look over the practice. Before you head out for the interview, make a list of questions you want to ask. What are your office hours? What would my hours be? What is your average daily patient load? Could you see the job description of the position you're interviewing for?

Talking About Salary

Your prospective employer is not the only one who stands to profit from your employment. You might love the profession and patients enough that you'd work as a volunteer, but most of us need a salary. Discussing salary is probably the most uncomfortable part of the interview from the interviewee's point of view. Many experts recommend that you not bring up the subject yourself, feeling that this makes you appear to be selfish and interested only in the cash. Not exactly the impression you want to make on a job interview! Obviously, however, you could not accept the position until salary is established.

So there you are. You are well-dressed, impeccably groomed, sitting comfortably straight, and leaning forward a little. Your face looks relaxed as you smile. Everyone's expectations seem to match, and things seem to be clicking. Then the doctor asks, "What kind of salary do you have in mind?"

How do you answer a question like that? You certainly don't want to undersell yourself. But neither do you want to price yourself out of a job.

There are several things you can do. First, do some research before the interview. Try to find out what other, similarly experienced, ophthalmic medical personnel make in that area of the country. Such survey information may be available through local or national organizations, or you can ask around. Next, consider your previous salary. In most cases you should better yourself with each new position. The exceptions would be if you have moved to a part of the country that is economically depressed, or if you change jobs frequently. Also take into consideration the skills you have that won't be required in the new position. For example, you may be certified in surgical assisting but are being interviewed for a position as an office technician who will never darken an operating room door. You have a valuable skill, but it is not one that the physician will pay you for because he or she doesn't need it.

Another suggestion is to look at your personal budget, decide what is the minimum you can afford to work for, and pad that a little to give yourself room for negotiating. (Remember to account for gas, child care, etc.)

If you can't come up with a figure for yourself, you might simply say, "Well, at my last job I was making _____." This knocks the question back to the physician/manager.

Traditional Benefits

Like with money, it is probably best not to ask about benefits at the first interview. You want the prospective employer to think about all that you have to offer the practice. Too much questioning on your part about salary and benefits sounds like you only want what's in it for you.

Yet benefits are something you need to know about before you agree to take the position. If, at the interview, you decide that you are genuinely interested in the job and no one brings up benefits, you might still be able to find out what you want to know. Ask the interviewer if you could see a copy of the practice's procedure manual. This is reasonable, and on one hand will allow you to familiarize yourself with what is expected of an employee. On the other hand, the manual should contain information on benefits. You find out what you want to know without asking

Table 6-1.

Benefits Checklist

Salary
Health and medical insurance
Retirement or investment plan
Continuing education allowance
Uniform allowance
Certification and recertification fees
Vacation time
Sick leave
Personal days
Association dues
Subscriptions to professional journals

directly and risking the appearance of being greedy. Table 6-1 is a check list of items you will want to identify and be clear on before you say "yes!"

Other Benefits

There is more to being employed than a salary and benefits, of course. Ask for a tour of the office. Notice everything! Here's a list to get you started:

Is the office clean? Safe?

Is the equipment in good shape?

Is the equipment relatively modern?

Is the equipment of the same type that you're used to using?

Is there enough physical room to accommodate another technician?

Does the doctor or manager introduce you to other employees? Are they friendly? Do they smile at you? At the boss? At the patients?

Was the reception area packed with patients when you came in?

Is the reception area clean, neat, pleasant, and roomy enough?

If you know someone who already works in the practice, talk to them. It would be great if you could speak to the employee you are replacing. Why is he or she leaving? What is the employee turnover rate? What is the doctor like to work for?

Even if you don't know someone in the practice and don't have access to the current employees, there is still a possibility of finding out what you want to know. If you ask among your friends and acquaintances, you're bound to find someone who is a patient of this practice. Then you can find out: Are the doctor and staff courteous? How long do you usually have to wait before being seen? A little prodding will probably get you all the information you need. But be tactful and word your questions carefully. If you pretend that the person you are questioning is the doctor's mother you'll be properly cautious and polite. "Word gets around" as they say. Assume that the office will hear that you've been asking around.

Interview Legalities

Because interviews carry legal implications, it is important that both interviewer and interviewee understand potential legal pitfalls. Specifically, they are as follows:

1. Avoid remarks that can be interpreted as discriminatory.
2. Remember that it is lawful to ask only job-related questions. Age, marital status, religious affiliation, etc. are not job-related questions.
3. Other discriminatory questions have to do with height and weight, hobbies or activities, sentiments, and disabilities or physical limitations.
4. Falsifying information can be grounds for dismissal.

If an interviewer asks you questions that fall into these categories, you must decide quickly how to respond. Being prepared ahead of time is even better. Examples of such questions include: "Are you married? Are you active in a local church? Where do you live? Do you have any children?" None of these are pertinent to the job itself.

It is true that these questions may be asked innocently as the interviewer seeks to initiate conversation and get to know you better. Unless the questions get too personal, you may decide to go ahead and answer. In addition, if you do respond, you might feel free to ask the interviewer the same type of questions. He or she is under no more obligation to answer than you are.

However, if you decide ahead of time to exercise your right to limit the discussion to job-related queries only, there are several ways to handle the situation. You might laugh off the question by chuckling and saying, "Oh, I didn't know living in town was a requirement for the job!" You haven't answered, you've made a subtle point, and you haven't been rude. Or, you may want to be more direct and simply ask, "Is that important to this position?" There may be a bona fide reason for asking, such as a nurse taking call and needing to be able to arrive at the hospital within a certain period of time.

If the interviewer can give no good reason for his or her line of questioning and continues to ask such questions, you may want to consider that this is not a place where you want to work.

Exiting the Interview

Concluding the interview is the last component of interviewing or getting the job. It is wise to never assume that you are going to receive immediate feedback. The following guidelines may help:
1. Bring closure on the decision so that both interviewer and interviewee understand where they are. Demonstrate this by summarizing and clarifying what has occurred.
2. Agree on a decision date where a yes or no answer would be given.
3. If possible, try to get it in writing.
4. Be polite and humble.
5. Remember to smile.

Chapter 7

Success, Advancement, and Certification

KEY POINTS

- You and you alone are responsible for your success.

- Write down your long-term goals. Then list the steps you need to take to achieve your goals.

- Success is not a destination; it is a process.

- Certification tells your employer and patients the value you place on what you do.

Your Real Boss

Every employee, whether management or not, wants to feel that he or she is appreciated for his or her efforts. Yet the sad truth is that only a small percentage (less than 5% of employees) truly get recognized for what they do and/or are promoted on the basis of merit. Typically, promotions in the eyecare field are more a result of happenstance than planning. Unprepared personnel are frequently thrust into positions of management without proper training. This creates a stressful situation where all the desire in the world to succeed may be, in fact, insufficient.

The key to success in eyecare is to understand some basic principles shared by all successful employees. They are as follows:

1. Know who your boss is.
2. Know what your boss wants.
3. Do it.

As simple as this may seem, it can be quite tricky. First, know who your boss is. Many employees make the mistake of thinking that their boss is their boss's boss or the owner of the practice. They are always trying to please the big boss by stopping by his or her office, engaging in chit chat, and offering suggestions. While attempting to socially engage with your boss may seem to be a good approach, it merely is a good way to get in trouble with your *real* boss who frequently will not appreciate your trying to go over his or her head. Your real boss may eventually have your head!

If for any reason you are not sure who your boss is, he or she is the one who hired you. It's the one who is responsible for setting your pay and the one who can recommend termination or actually fire you. He or she may also be the one who has been frowning at you.

Second, know what your boss wants. Your boss will tell you what he or she wants if you listen. In fact, if necessary, your boss will tell you more than once. But eventually, your boss will get tired of having to tell you.

Third, do it! You have your ideas of how your job ought to be done. Bosses have their own ideas. Do it the boss's way. Show the boss that you can do the job. The boss will be pleased, perhaps even surprised, and will come to trust you. When the boss trusts your judgment, he or she will begin to let you try your own ideas of how the job ought to be done. The end result is a covenant or a pact between you and your boss. This is frequently unwritten but it goes like this: You make your boss look good and the boss takes care of you. You couldn't ask for anything better. The boss couldn't either.

Rising to the Top

Aside from understanding the above-mentioned rules, the next most important element is to realize that you and you alone are responsible for your success. The most successful employees look into the mirror and say these words out loud, "If it is to be, it is up to me." Upper management will always look for the rising stars, the people who are taking responsibility for themselves and their own success.

Another principle of attaining success is to understand that in order to be successful, you must be prepared to work at least one-half of a day . . . and you get to choose which 12 hours that is.

The next precept deals with the law of winners and losers. Winners always do what losers don't want to do. This means planning, preparation, and a strong sense of purpose.

One of the keys to achieving advancement is to call attention to yourself so that you will easily be identified as one who possesses the desirable characteristics of long-term employment and advancement. Thus, the laws for success dictate, "Ye shall know how to communicate and conduct yourself so that you are a desirable entity." This means adopting and living by the following tenets:

1. Walk your talk. Let others see that you always become what you say you are. You embrace it, live it, and walk it every day.
2. Be consistent. Stand up for your rights and hold firm to your beliefs. Never waiver from what you believe.
3. Choose your words carefully.

The six most important words: "I admit I made a mistake."

The five most important words: "You did a good job."

The four most important words: "What is your opinion?"

The three most important words: "If you please."

The two most important words: "Thank you."

The most important word: "We."

The least important word: "I."

Setting Goals

In order to become the best that you can be, you must clearly understand what it is that you desire. The difference between desires and wants is the difference between objectives and dreams. If your goals are not written, then they are nothing more than dreams. The following steps will give you a clearer vision of what it is that you want:

1. First, list all the things you would like to accomplish. Now rank them in order of importance. Include a description of how you would like to look to others.
2. Ask yourself what are the first two steps you need to take to achieve each goal.
3. In the art of goal setting, it is important to look at both short-term and long-term goals. Frequently it is the long-range goals that start up the element of short-term planning which is, in fact, nothing more than the details of achieving the long-term goal itself.

Example: (Long-term goal) I will be promoted within a year.

Example: (Short-term goal) I will do one specific thing each day in order to get recognized.

Day 1. I will look for one additional task to do, assuming I have finished my own work.

Day 2. I will make it a point to compliment my fellow workers for being part of a team with me.

Day 3. I will go out of my way to assist a fellow worker.

In this manner, you will begin to move in a positive direction toward your ultimate goal.

What Happens

The next major principle in achieving success is to understand that pressure is normal, but stress is self-created. (We'll discuss stress in more detail in the next chapter.) The key here is to realize that it is not what happens to you that is important, it's what you do with what happens to you that is important. Thus, any negative experience can be found to have positive aspects. Winners learn from their mistakes while losers are doomed to repeat them. Here are ten good rules for succeeding at being human:

1. *You have a body.* You may like it or hate it, but it will be yours for the duration.
2. *You will learn lessons.* You are enrolled in a full-time informal school called *life.* Each day in this school you will have the opportunity to learn lessons. You may like the lessons or think them irrelevant and stupid.
3. *There are no mistakes, only lessons.* Growth is a process of trial and error and experimentation. The "failed" experiments are as much a part of the process as the experiment that ultimately "works."
4. *A lesson is repeated until learned.* A lesson will be presented to you in various forms until you have learned it. When you have learned it, you can go on to the next lesson.
5. *Learning lessons does not end.* There is no part of life that does not contain its lessons. If you are alive, there are lessons to be learned.
6. *"There" is no better than "here."* When your "there" becomes a "here," you will simply obtain another "there" that will again look better than "here."
7. *Others are merely mirrors of you.* You cannot love or hate something about another person unless it reflects something you love or hate about yourself.
8. *What you make of your life is up to you.* You have all the tools and resources you need. What you do with them is up to you.
9. *You will forget all of this.*
10. *You can remember it whenever you want!*

Once the responsibility for one's own success is accepted, it is easy to understand and apply the following laws of success:

1. It is not what is said to you that is important, it's what you say to yourself after the other person has stopped speaking. That's what is important.
2. Nobody can make you mad without your permission.
3. No one can upset you without your allowing it.
4. There are always choices.

Winners in eyecare are those who follow these principles:

1. Choose to listen to the positive rather than the negative. When faced with the negative, dismiss it in favor of focusing on the positive.
2. Associate with people who are positive and who are already successful.
3. Spend at least one-half hour a day reading and learning about the business you are in.
4. Spend an equal amount of time on self-development and read inspirational literature books, listen to tapes, and view leadership material.
5. Understand that success is not a destination. It is a process.

Certification

The eyecare field is vast. It provides many opportunities for motivated persons to advance. Some of the specialty areas in eyecare are:

- Paraoptometry
- Ophthalmic medical personnel
- Orthoptist
- Surgical assisting
- Low vision
- Photography
- Ophthalmic ultrasonography

- Contact lenses
- Eye banking
- Ophthalmic nursing
- Opticianry
- Ocularistry

Paraoptometry

The American Optometric Association, Paraoptometric Section, offers two levels of certification: Optometric Assistant (OptA) and Optometric Technician (OptT). One must qualify to take the written exam at either level by working in the field, obtaining prescribed education (through meetings or the Home Study Course for Optometric Assisting), or serving in optometry in the military, or completing a recognized formal program. Because OptT is the more advanced level, more is required in order to qualify to take the exam.

Exam criteria for the OptA includes Practice Management, Ophthalmic Optics and Dispensing, Basic Procedures, Special Procedures, Refractive Status, and Basic Ocular Anatomy and Physiology.

The exam for certification as an OptT covers pretesting procedures, clinical procedures, ophthalmic optics and dispensing, refractive status of the eye and binocularity, anatomy and physiology, and practice management.

The information given here is taken from the most recent data available prior to publication. For information on the home study course and to obtain a handbook for the examinations, contact:

American Optometric Association
ParaOptometric Section
243 North Lindbergh Boulevard
St. Louis, MO 63141-7881
phone: 1-314-991-4100
fax: 1-314-991-4101

In addition to the home study course, there are other study materials available for those who wish to prepare for examinations. Two that are worth looking into are *Opticianry: The Practice and the Art,* Volumes I through IV, and the *Successful Optical Sales* (audio-cassette series) by Bill Borover, both available from Gracie Enterprises, PO Box 506, Chula Vista, CA 91912. In addition, the *Basic Bookshelf for Eyecare Professionals* was written to include all of the exam content areas one needs to review for the tests. Information needed by each certification level is pointed out in the margin of the series books. Series titles *Ophthalmic Assistant Exam Review* and *Ophthalmic Technician Exam Review,* which can also be obtained through SLACK Incorporated, each contain an appendix to refer OptA and OptT exam takers to questions that pertain to their exams as well.

Ophthalmic Medical Personnel

Those assisting in ophthalmology, generically known as ophthalmic medical personnel (OMP), can be certified at three levels: certified ophthalmic assistant (COA®), certified ophthalmic technician (COT®), and certified ophthalmic medical technologist (COMT®). Their certifying body is the Joint Commission on Allied Health Personnel in Ophthalmology® (JCAHPO®).

Those who wish to take the examinations in ophthalmology must first qualify. One option is

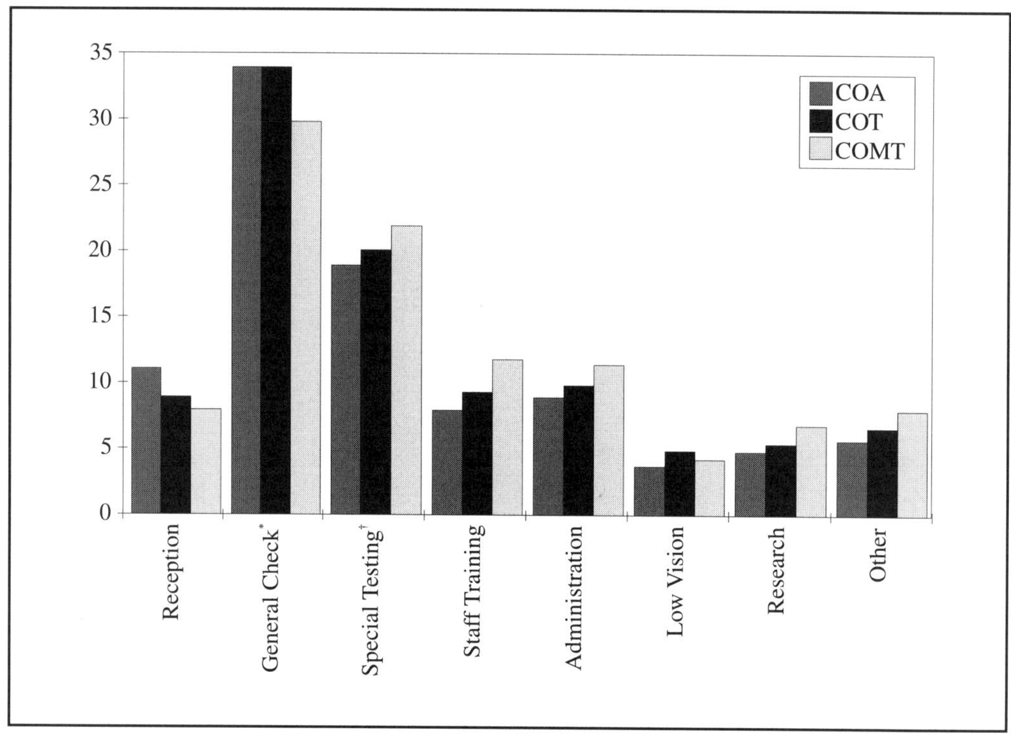

Figure 7-1. Time spent in general areas of responsibility.
*Includes tasks identified as "patient screening."
†Includes such tasks as perimetry, A-scan, specular microscopy.
(Reprinted by permission: Woodworth K. E., Campbell R. C., Dean C. A. et al. Analysis of Tasks Performed by Certified Ophthalmic Medical Personnel. *Ophthalmology.* Philadelphia, PA: Lippincott-Raven Publishers; 1995;102(12): 1973-1986. Copyright by the American Academy of Ophthalmology, Inc.)

to enroll in a formal training program leading to the desired credential. Most OMP, however, are job trained. In this case, you may qualify by working in the field for a specified length of time. Your physician sponsor must sign a form indicating that you are proficient at certain tasks. You must hold current cardiopulmonary resuscitation credentials. At the COA® level, one must first take and pass the Home Study Course developed by the American Academy of Ophthalmology (AAO). At the COT® and COMT® levels, increasing amounts of approved continuing education credits are required. In addition, once the candidate has passed the written exam for COT® or COMT®, a practical exam must be taken as well. In order to keep one's credentials, proof of continuing education must be submitted. Continuing education credits are given for JCAHPO®-approved classes and self-study.

The exam at the COA® level includes questions covering history taking, basic skills and lensometry, patient services, basic tonometry, instrument maintenance, general medical knowledge, and special studies (A-scan).

The prospective COT® exam covers COA®-level material as well as special studies (fundus photography), clinical optics, basic ocular motility, visual fields, contact lenses, intermediate tonometry, and ocular pharmacology. The skills evaluation (practical exam) includes lensometry, retinoscopy, refractometry, muscle testing, nonautomated visual field testing, keratometry, and simulated applanation tonometry.

Candidates for the COMT® level are tested on the COA® and COT® content areas in addition to microbiology, advanced tonometry, advanced visual fields, advanced color vision, advanced clinical optics, advanced ocular motility, photography, advanced pharmacology, special instruments and techniques, and advanced general medical knowledge. During the practical exam, they must perform calibrations, tests, and identifications in each of the above advanced areas. (Details are given in the criteria booklet).

Recently a study was done by JCAHPO® to evaluate the types of activities that certified OMP perform at various levels (Figure 7-1). In addition, a survey was conducted wherein individuals in the three certification levels, as well as their sponsoring physicians, ranked 77 tasks commonly performed by OMP. The results are given in Table 7-1. (It is important to know that for the purposes of the JCAHPO® study, the term OMP referred only to *certified* personnel.)

Across the board, there was agreement in the ranking of the five most important tasks (history taking, patient instruction, visual acuity, ocular medications, and applanation tonometry) among the OMP and physicians. The rating of the remaining tasks was very close between the two groups as well. The results from the study have been used to update the content areas for the certification exams. In addition, physician employers can use the data to evaluate the level of tasks that their OMP are performing.

To contact JCAHPO® about the exam criteria or a reprint of the full task analysis survey, you may write or call:

JCAHPO®
2025 Woodlane Drive
St. Paul, MN 55125-2995
phone: 1-800-284-3937
For the ophthalmic assisting home study course, contact:
AAO
PO Box 7424
San Francisco, CA 94120
phone: 1-415-561-8500
fax: 1-415-561-8533

Other Certifications

Besides the foundational duties performed by certified optometric and ophthalmic personnel, there are areas of specialty to be explored. Because of space limitations, we will not go into much detail. Instead we will give a brief description of the type of work involved and the agency to contact for more information.

Certified Orthoptist

Orthoptists diagnose and manage amblyopia and strabismus under the supervision of an ophthalmologist. To obtain information about eligibility for the written and practical examinations, contact:

Leslie France, CO, COT
c/o The American Orthoptic Council
3914 Nakoma Road
Madison, WI 53711
phone: 1-608-233-5383

Table 7-1.

Time Spent in General Areas of Responsibility

Description	Rank Given by:				
	COA®	COT®	COMT®	OMP	MD
History taking	1	1	2	1	1
Instructing patients	2	3	4	3	3
Measuring acuity	3	2	1	2	2
Ocular medications	4	4	8	4	4
Applanation tonometry	5	5	5	5	5
Assisting minor surgery	6	8	23	6	8
Minor surgery instrument preparation	7	10	22	8	9
Testing pupils	8	6	6	7	10
Automated perimetry	9	12	24	11	7
A-scan	10	9	18	9	6
Changing batteries/bulbs	11	13	10	12	13
Manual lensometer	12	11	9	13	12
Amsler grid	13	14	15	14	15
Refining refractive error	14	7	3	10	11
Eye dressings	15	16	35	16	20
Contrast sensitivity	16	17	29	17	18
Minor repairs	17	15	16	15	17
Maintaining inventory	18	22	33	18	27
Laser therapy assisting	19	21	40	21	26
Color vision HRR	20	20	20	20	21
Cleaning Goldmann tonometer, etc.	21	19	17	19	16
Automated lensometer	22	25	45	22	19
Clerical duties	23	37	56	28	38
Identifying medications	24	27	31	24	25
Confrontation field	25	23	19	23	22
Sterilizing instruments	26	28	32	27	29
Fundus photography	27	24	30	26	23
Supervised automated perimetry	28	30	48	29	24
Visual acuity special (ie, low vision)	29	33	38	32	40
Administrative	30	29	27	30	32
Assisting the surgeon	31	32	36	33	30
Retinoscopy	32	18	7	25	28
Automated refractometer	33	46	64	41	41
Stereoacuity	34	31	14	34	31
Cover-uncover test	35	26	11	31	34
Sterile procedures	36	39	37	36	35
Instruct patients on contact lens insertion and removal	37	40	41	38	37
Version/duction	38	34	12	35	33
Fluorescein angiography	39	35	42	37	36
Corneal curvature	40	36	43	39	14

Table 7-1.

Time Spent in General Areas of Responsibility (continued)

Description	Rank Given by:				
	COA®	COT®	COMT®	OMP	MD
Goldmann perimeter	41	38	28	40	39
Schirmer tear test	42	48	57	46	45
Tonography	43	49	58	47	74
Corneal specimens	44	54	51	49	48
Anterior segment photography	45	41	47	42	42
Scrub nurse duties	46	47	46	45	43
Near point of accommodation	47	45	25	44	49
Near point of convergence	48	44	21	43	44
B-scan	49	51	52	51	54
Color vision Farnsworth	50	61	61	54	62
Suture removal	51	52	59	52	55
Bowl perimeter	52	42	34	48	46
Air-puff tonometer	53	62	66	60	52
Corneal diameter	54	58	60	59	57
Worth 4-Dot	55	53	26	53	51
Phacoemulsifier, etc.	56	56	54	56	50
Interpupillary distance	57	57	49	58	61
Measuring contact lenses	58	55	53	57	53
Measuring deviations with prisms	59	43	13	50	47
Cleaning Schiotz tonometer, etc.	60	59	62	61	56
Vertex distance	61	50	39	55	58
Specular photography	62	60	55	62	60
Tangent screen	63	63	50	63	59
Culture on plates	64	69	67	65	67
Schiotz tonometer	65	65	63	66	63
Polish contact lenses	66	67	65	67	65
Exophthalmometry	67	64	44	64	64
Low-vision magnifiers	68	66	68	68	66
Darkroom procedures	69	68	69	69	68
Low-vision telescopic	70	70	70	70	69
Provocative tests	71	72	74	72	71
Gram/Giemsa stains	72	74	73	73	75
Ophthalmodynamometry	73	71	72	71	70
ERG, EOG, VER/VEP	74	73	71	74	72
Identify bacteria	75	76	75	75	76
Dark adaptation	76	75	76	76	73
Minor adjustments	77	77	77	77	77

COA® = certified ophthalmic assistant; COT® = certified ophthalmic technician; COMT® = certified ophthalmic medical technologist; OMP = ophthalmic medical personnel; MD = medical doctor; HRR = Hardy-Rand-Rittler; ERG = electroretinogram; EOG = electro-oculogram; VER = visual evoked response; VEP = visual evoked potential.
(Reprinted by permission: Woodworth K. E., Campbell R. C., Dean C. A., et al. Analysis of Tasks Performed by Certified Ophthalmic Medical Personnel. Ophthalmology. *Philadelphia, PA: Lippincott-Raven Publishers; 1995;102(12): 1973-1986. Copyright by the American Academy of Ophthalmology, Inc)*

Ophthalmic Surgical Assisting Subspecialty

This credential was created by JCAHPO® for those who assist with eye surgery. Information on the written exam is available from JCAHPO® (refer to page 77).

Low Vision Subspecialty

Certification in low vision is a newer credential developed by JCAHPO®. Applicants must be knowledgeable in the selection and dispensing of low vision aids, as well as patient education. For a booklet on the exam write to JCAHPO® (refer to page 77).

Certified Retinal Angiographer and Certified Ophthalmic Photographer and Retinal Angiographer

Because the eye's interior can be seen from the outside, ophthalmic photography is a key diagnostic modality. Eligibility for the two available levels includes assembling a portfolio of one's work. One must pass both written and practical exams. For more information, contact:

Barbara McCalley, Membership Office
c/o Ophthalmic Photographer's Society
213 Lorene
Nixa, MO 65714-9230
phone: 1-417-725-0181

Registered Diagnostic Medical Sonographer, Ophthalmology

There are two types of ultrasound used in ophthalmology: A-scan (usually used to measure axial length) and B-scan (which gives a real-time computer image of the eye's interior). To become registered, one must pass an exam on sonography in general (ultrasound physics and instrumentation), then another specialty test on ophthalmic ultrasound. For more information, contact:

American Registry of Diagnostic Medical Sonographers
Donald Gardiner, Executive Director
600 Jefferson Plaza, Suite 360
Rockville, MD 20852-1150
phone: 1-800-541-9754

Certified Contact Lens Technician

The contact lens technician fits and dispenses contacts under the supervision of an optometrist or ophthalmologist, depending on state law. Information on the certification exam can be obtained from:

American Board of Opticianry
National Contact Lens Examiners
10341 Democracy Lane
Fairfax, VA 22030-2521
phone: 1-703-691-8356
fax: 1-703-691-3929

(The Contact Lens Association of Ophthalmologists [CLAO] offers a home study course for contact lens technicians, available by calling 1-800-783-5355. The course itself does not lead to a specific credential, but is valuable for study.)

Certified Eye Bank Technician

These eye banking specialists are trained to harvest and preserve ocular tissue for research and donor programs. One must pass a written and practical examination. For information on the examination, contact:

Patricia Aiken-O'Neal, President
Eye Bank Association of America
1001 Connecticut Ave. NW, Suite 601
Washington, DC 20036
phone: 1-202-775-4999

Certified Registered Nurse in Ophthalmology

Registered Nurses who are currently licensed in the United States and have experience in ophthalmology may apply to take the exam. For more information, contact:

Jodi-Ann Nakayama, Client Services Coordinator
c/o American Society of Ophthalmic Registered Nurses
PO Box 193030
San Francisco, CA 94119
phone: 1-415-561-8513

Certified Optician

Opticians are involved in frame selection and fitting, lens preparation, dispensing frames and lenses, and dispensing contact lenses. In order to be a *licensed* optician, one must apply for a license in accordance with your state's requirements. For information on certification, write to the American Board of Opticianry (refer to page 80).

Certified Ocularist

An ocularist is involved with fitting ocular prostheses (artificial eyes). In addition to training and instruction, one must pass both written and practical exams. For more information, contact:

David Bulgarelli, Executive Director
National Examining Board of Ocularists
625 First Avenue, Suite 220
Coralville, IA 52241
phone: 1-319-354-3434

Professional Organizations

Additionally, each of these specialty groups have society memberships, newsletters, publications, etc., which can be accessed through most eyecare offices. The certifying bodies themselves often have information on national, state, and local organizations. These groups are a great way to network with your professional peers, influence your profession, and keep up with the latest technology and education. (Membership also looks good on a résumé!)

An ancient Chinese proverb says when the student is ready, the teacher will appear.

Chapter 8

Stress and Burnout

KEY POINTS

- You are what you think.

- It's not what happens to you that's important, it's what you do with what happens to you that's important.

- The key to preventing burnout is to control stress.

- Burnout is the result of situations causing frustration over achieving goals in relationships or jobs.

The terms stress and burnout have been used simultaneously and generally represent a state of anguish where the person experiencing the symptoms simply can't handle it any more. From a more practical point of view, stress is little more than the transfer of emotional feelings (usually negative) to physical manifestations. Thus, when emotional feelings produce physical maladies such as headaches, nausea, fatigue, boredom, loss of concentration, etc., it is frequently a reaction to stress that can eventually lead to total burnout.

Whereas one could spend a great deal of time trying to define stress, it is more important to understand what stress does. Stress can create bad feelings, poor performance, and, in its most advanced state, paralysis of action (burnout).

You Are What You Think

Developing the tools to deal with stress begins with understanding that it is not what happens to you that's important, it's what you *do* with what happens to you that's important. The truth is that no one can make you feel badly or hurt your feelings without your permission. Thought truly is everything and we are what we think about most of the time. These platitudes are easy to say but difficult to internalize and accept. The following exercise will prove that thought is the root of all feelings.

Imagine yourself in a room with 20 other people. A giant measuring stick (pupillary distance ruler) is laid out on the floor in front of you. This giant ruler is 1 inch thick, 12 inches wide and exactly 20 feet (6 meters) in length. The team leader places a hundred dollar bill at one end of the plank and challenges you to walk across the plank, pick up the hundred dollar bill, and walk back. Then the prize is yours. The question is, would you do it?

For most normal human beings this would be a relatively simple task, and the participant would most likely perform a little curtsy at the end, wondering if the initiator might want to go for two.

Now imagine this same plank suspended between two buildings. The leader again places a one hundred dollar bill on the end of the plank and this time places a little rock on top of it to keep it from fluttering away in the wind. He invites you once again to walk the plank, pick up the one hundred dollar bill, and walk back, keeping the prize. Would you do it now?

Most normal human beings begin to feel their palms sweating at this point in time and would answer with an emphatic "No!" But why?

The reason that the participants would take the challenge in the first scenario and not take it in the second is because in the first scenario they can visualize themselves succeeding. In the second scenario they can "see" themselves failing (ie, falling, getting hurt, taking too much of a risk, etc.). As human beings, we all move away from painful things and move toward pleasurable ones. The point is that there was absolutely no difference in your physical capabilities when it came to walking the plank, picking up the one hundred dollar bill, and walking back in either scenario. Therefore, the only thing that made the difference was thought.

If thought is everything, then the control of thought can produce wanted feelings and/or emotion. When it comes to dealing with fellow workers, this principle can be applied at one more level: it is not what is said to you that's important, but rather what you say to yourself once the other person stops speaking. That's essential! The inner voice which resides inside all of us is the real person of our being. This inner person has the real scoop on how we think we are. For example: If you have a relatively low opinion of yourself, you tend to think you deserve to be abased. In fact, there are psychological studies that prove that as human beings we tend to act out how we really feel about ourselves as people from the standpoint of self-worth and self-esteem.

Whereas there are numerous books, tapes, and other resources for helping one understand his or her psychological makeup, the point is to develop techniques so that negative emotions are minimized and production is maximized. Self-acceptance is the key.

Accept yourself as you are, not as you think other people perceive you. To find out how far you are along the path to the ultimate self-development, look into the mirror when you are alone, and while maintaining direct eye contact, say these words, "I accept myself 100% exactly as I am." Say it twice, then listen for the inner voice to go off. If the inner voice says such things as "Well, I'll accept myself 100% exactly as I am when I achieve my ideal weight goal, or when I get my degree, or when I get rid of this significant other, or when my hair grows back, etc.," then you have learned an invaluable insight. And you have some work to do!

Dealing With Stress

To handle stress successfully you must do something when it appears rather than merely accept it as something you must bear. Here are some rules for dealing with stress:

1. Accept the fact that some people will intentionally try to make you feel bad.
2. You, and you alone, are responsible for how you feel.
3. Positive thoughts beget positive feelings.
4. Every single day offers you a menu. You and you alone can choose whether it is going to be a good day or a bad one.
5. "Hang out" with positive people. If people around you are negative, then refuse to participate in their thoughts. Continue to believe in your positive ones.
6. When feeling pressure, try to get away to a quiet spot and relax. This could be at lunch, during breaks, or after work. The important thing is to develop time for yourself to deal with your feelings.

When there is no time to relax try the wonderful "swoosh" technique, developed by Dr. Richard Bandler in *Reframing: Neurolinguistic Programming* published by Real People Press in 1981. Using this method is easy because all it requires is to picture a basketball traveling through the air and then "swooshing" to make a basket. While the ball is in the air you are feeling the negative emotion. You tell yourself that once the ball descends through the hoop making the "swoosh" sound, the emotion will change immediately. Here is an example:

You are at work and someone thoughtlessly snubs you or treats you rudely. Feeling the emotion of anger, you immediately picture yourself shooting a basketball through the air and waiting for it to "swoosh." The moment the imaginary ball exits the hoop, you have a smile on your face and are very understanding and forgiving of other people's inadequacies. This is the essence of using the "swoosh" technique. Perhaps once you master it, you can teach other people to use it also.

Unrelieved stress can lead to burnout, which we'll cover next. However, it makes sense that if we apply burnout recovery methods to stress, perhaps we can avoid burnout. Here are more suggestions:

- Get enough rest.
- Exercise regularly.
- Eat a healthy diet.
- Examine your priorities regularly.
- Make time to relax and play.
- Pay attention to what your body is trying to tell you.

Burnout

"Burning the candle at both ends." You might get more light that way, but the candle will be used up twice as fast. It is also a good definition of the path to burnout.

Burnout can be defined as the frustration and exhaustion that results when events conspire to block the desired results of a relationship or job. It is not just a malady of so-called high achievers, but can strike anyone who is seeking to reach a goal (whether the goal is verbalized or not). It is true, however, that goal-oriented people are the most commonly afflicted. Burnout can reduce a person with the most energetic, positive outlook into a person who can't choose bananas at the grocery store...or perhaps doesn't even have the energy to leave the house to go to the store.

Burnout Lists

The following information is gleaned from Myron Rush's excellent book *Burnout: Practical Help for Lives Out of Balance* published in 1989 by Victor Books of Wheaton, IL.

The ten most common causes of burnout:
Feeling driven instead of called
Failing to pace yourself
Trying to do it all yourself
Excessive contact with people's problems
Majoring on the minors
Unrealistic expectations
Developing too many routines
Skewed priorities
Poor physical condition
Continuous rejection
External symptoms of burnout:
Increased activity without increased productivity
Irritability
Physical fatigue
Unwillingness to risk
Internal symptoms of burnout:
Loss of courage
Loss of personal identity and self-worth
Loss of objectivity
Emotional exhaustion
Negative mental attitude
Consequences of burnout:
Loss of purpose in life
Destruction of self-image
Feeling alone
Resentment and bitterness
Hopelessness

Dealing With Burnout

From the severity of some of the items in the above lists, you can see that a person with burnout is going to need some help. The assistance that is necessary is probably not going to be available from the employer, the office manager, or the coworkers. Mr. Rush says that even the most strong-willed person (and he includes himself in that group) cannot overcome burnout's lack of motivation and energy in order to help himself or herself. Professional counseling is probably going to be required.

Once in counseling, Myron Rush has two principles to offer a person who is recovering from burnout: don't expect too much too soon, and don't expect things to be like they were before. Benefits of recovery include learning to work smarter, not harder, as well as learning how to pace yourself instead of drive yourself.

A counsellor who is experienced in helping burned-out people will probably offer some of the following advice:

- Give yourself some distance from the source of the burnout. If you can take a vacation, do it. If not, perhaps you can request a change of department or a change of duties.
- Include time for rest and relaxation in your life. This can be difficult for high-achievers to do. You feel like you can't afford to take some time for play. But given the shape you're in now and the direction you're going, can you really afford *not* to? Do something just for fun, and don't think or talk about your problems while you're doing it.
- To begin rebuilding your self-confidence, set some short-range goals that you can successfully complete. "Short-range" is the key here. It might be as simple as smiling in the morning when you walk in the office door. You might not feel like doing it, but you can do it. And when you do it, you must call it a success and congratulate yourself.
- Establish a regular exercise routine.

Helping Burned-Out Employees

A supervisor can help employees first by keeping tabs on the stress level of the office, and second, by becoming familiar with the burnout lists given above. Here are some hints on how to help a burned-out employee:

- Create opportunities for small, immediate successes.
- Work with the employee to provide some time to get away, whether it is a vacation or a change in job responsibilities, shift, or department.
- Suggest outside counseling if you feel it is appropriate.
- Don't compromise company standards to accommodate a burned-out employee who refuses help.

Remember that even though he or she may be paralyzed by burnout at the moment, the employee is still familiar with your practice and your patients. Rehabilitation is worth it!

Legal Issues

- The patient is the most important person in the practice.

- Any gross dissatisfaction, threat to bring legal action, or incident that could possibly result in legal action should be documented and brought to the physician's attention at once.

- The Good Samaritan Law varies from state to state and is designed to protect both victims and medically trained rescuers.

Patient Rights

Every interaction on behalf of the eyecare practice carries with it a consequence. This consequence can be positive or negative. Positive consequences are those interactions that impart information and communication without endangering the rights of the most important person within the practice—the patient.

The Patient's Bill of Rights

1. The patient has the right to considerate and respectful care.
2. The patient has the right to obtain from his or her physician complete current information concerning the diagnosis, treatment, and prognosis in terms the patient can reasonably understand. When it is not medically advisable to give such information to the patient, the information should be made available to an appropriate person on his or her behalf. The patient has the right to know, by name, the physician responsible for coordinating his or her care.
3. The patient has the right to receive from his or her physician information necessary to give informed consent prior to the start of any procedure and/or treatment. Except in emergencies, such information for informed consent should include, but not necessarily be limited to, the specific procedure and/or treatment, the medically significant risks involved, and the probable duration of incapacitation. Where medically significant alternatives for care or treatment exist, or when the patient requests information concerning medical alternatives, he or she has the right to such information. The patient also has the right to know the name of the person responsible for the procedures and/or treatment.
4. The patient has the right to refuse treatment to the extent permitted by law and to be informed of the medical consequences of his or her action.
5. The patient has the right to every consideration of his or her privacy concerning his or her own medical care program. Case discussion, consultation, examination, and treatment are confidential and should be conducted discreetly. Staff not directly involved in the patient's care must have the patient's permission to be present.
6. The patient has the right to expect that all communications and records pertaining to his or her care should be treated as confidential.
7. The patient has the right to obtain information as to any relationship of the eye center to other health care and educational institutions insofar as his or her care is concerned. The patient has the right to obtain information as to the existence of any professional relationships among individuals, by name, who are treating him or her.
8. The patient has the right to examine and receive an explanation of his or her bill regardless of the source of the payment.

Avoiding Litigation

Most doctor's medical malpractice insurance also covers employees. You need to verify this by speaking with your supervisor or directly with your doctor.

With regard to performing diagnostics and clinical assisting, it is extremely important to represent yourself as a physician extender and not an eye doctor. If the patient perceives you as having given them medical advice, it compromises the medical/legal relationship. Instead, develop the habit of speaking to the patient in the third person rather than the first person. For example, say, "Dr. Borover will be happy to know that you read all the way down to the 20/25 line today," rather than, "I'm glad to see that you have read all the way down to the 20/20 line today."

Here are eight rules for protecting the patient's rights and avoiding potential litigation:

1. The patient actually owns the information in the chart. The practice owns the paper the information is printed on. The information in the patient's chart (medical record) is confidential. Any release of this information without the patient's express permission is illegal. When patients ask about their records, it is important for them to understand that you are not trying to withhold the information, but you may not legally give it without an authorized signature. From time to time, someone other than the patient, such as a relative or attorney, may request information on behalf of the patient. In this instance, the same guidelines must be followed with regard to a signed Request for Records Release (Form 1, Appendix). In the case of minors, a parent or guardian must apply for the information.

2. It is unprofessional to discuss patient's medical conditions amongst staff and immoral to discuss it outside of the practice. It is very common for employees to discuss the day's activities and even remark on some of the people they have come into contact with. In a professional practice, however, this can lead to problems if it ever came to pass that the patient's medical conditions have been divulged without their express authorization.

3. Documentation in the chart should remain unaltered and never obliterated. If an error has occurred and needs to be corrected, the correct procedure is to strike a line through the flawed text and write the correction in the margin. All corrections in charts should be initialed by the person who made the correction. Medical records that are correctly documented are frequently what saves the doctor in a lawsuit.

4. Any threat of a lawsuit or of gross dissatisfaction on the patient's part should be reported to the doctor immediately.

5. Any incident that might conceivably become litigious should be documented and brought to the attention of the physician. One good mechanism for tracking this is to use an "incident" report (Form 11, Appendix). An incident report documents a particular event without any editorializing. This incident report should then be filed in the patient's chart. For example: August 8, 1996: Patient slipped and fell to the ground. The clinical supervisor, Mary McGaha, helped her to a chair and asked her if she was okay. The patient responded, "Yes, I just lost my footing." Any additional action on the physician's part should be written on the report as well, such as: "Dr. Borover suggested that the patient have an x-ray of her left ankle. The patient said she felt that was not necessary."

6. Be careful when you attempt to reassure a patient. It is tempting to tell a distraught injured patient that "everything will be just fine." Your only intent is to offer comfort. But if the patient later looses the eye, he or she could conceivably sue because of a guaranteed "fine" outcome. Instead, you might tell the patient, "Dr. Borover will do everything he can to help you."

7. Always praise in public. Criticize in private. Patients are acutely aware of other people in an eye doctor's office. Because visiting an eye doctor is a relatively scary event, it is easy for patients to misinterpret and think that the staff is talking about them. Patients should never overhear the staff discussing a problem, as they may

think they are the cause of it or at least a part of it. This makes the patient unhappy and dissatisfied, and may cause a litigious atmosphere. Anytime negative comments are made, it should always be done in strict privacy.

8. Never practice medicine without a license.

    a. Do not diagnose. Even though you know what it is the patient has, never volunteer it. Learn the art of verbal self-defense. If the patient asks, "What do I have?" Answer with, "The interpretation and treatment of disease is the doctor's job. He or she will be happy to discuss this with you."

    b. You may not legally write an optical prescription. You may perform refractometry, the measuring of the patient's refractive error. However, you may not do a refraction, which involves taking the refractometric measurement, applying clinical judgment, and arriving at a prescription.

    c. Do not offer an opinion. Always defer to the doctor by saying, "This is a matter that only the doctor can talk about. He has asked me to collect this information for him."

    d. Do not interpret diagnostic findings. For example, rather than saying, "Your eye pressure is on the high side today," say, "Dr. Borover will look at these numbers and interpret them for you."

Legal Terms

Abandonment is failure to attend to a patient who has not been discharged. The physician may dismiss a patient with reasonable advanced notice and not be guilty of abandonment. Such a notice must include not only a sensible length of time in which the patient may find another physician, but also an assessment of the patient's condition and needs for future treatment.

A *breach of contract* is failure to produce promised results.

Liability is that for which you are legally responsible.

Malpractice is patient injury that is due to negligence, ignorance, carelessness, or criminal intent on the part of a health practitioner in the rendering of professional medical services.

Negligence is performance that is below the legal standard of care.

Standard of care (acceptable or customary practice) is the expected level of performance of a competent physician.

Vicarious liability is a situation in which an innocent party is held liable for the actions of a second party (for example, a physician employer is named in a suit where his assistant divulged private patient records).

Good Samaritans

From time to time there are accidents or incidents outside the office that are addressed by eyecare professionals or the eyecare team. When trying to help an injured person in an emergency situation, it is comforting to remember the Good Samaritan Law. The law was written to encourage trained medical individuals to provide emergency care with immunity from any civil complaint for negligence. By its very nature, the Good Samaritan Law also protects the victim from unauthorized or unprofessional help. The details vary from state to state. Laws in some states cover physicians only while others include other medical personnel. States differ on their requirements that you:

1. Are part of the class of persons granted immunity,
2. have a "good faith" state of mind,
3. do not receive payment for your emergency care,
4. are rendering aid in a location approved by the state (which may or may not include your office when the physician is not there) and,
5. comply to a minimum acceptable standard of care.

Any attempt to help an injured patient outside of the practice could be looked on as being performed on behalf of the practice. To prevent the victim from interpreting your assistance as an extension of your employer and practice, remove any identifying items (such as an embroidered lab coat or an office name tag) before rendering care.

We all want to help others, especially those in distress. It's too bad that we have to weigh our desire to assist with our fear of being sued. But remember, you may not be obligated to the victim until you actually begin to render aid. For example, you know cardiopulmonary resuscitation (CPR) but are not obligated to perform it. However, once you start CPR you are obligated to continue it until a) the patient regains heartbeats and respirations, b) another qualified person takes over, or c) there is no one to help and you are too exhausted to continue. An exception to this "not obligated" status occurs in states with duty to aid laws.

If You Are Named in a Lawsuit

Understanding the pitfalls of working in the health care field helps protect both yourself and your eye doctor. What happens if you are named in a lawsuit? Here is a check list of action items regarding getting sued:

1. Relax and stay calm. Just because a lawsuit is intended does not mean it will actually occur or the suer will win.
2. Do not call the patient or speak to the patient's attorney without your attorney being present.
3. Contact your professional liability carrier and ask for further instructions.
4. Tell no one, not even your own family.
5. Isolate the patient's records and store them in a safe place. Photocopy another set for safekeeping.
6. Never change or add anything to the records, even though you think it may help you or your doctor.

A Final Note

"All this legal talk takes the fun out of my job. All I want to do is help people see better."

Is that what you're thinking? It is unfortunate that we have to be so cautious when our goal is so worthy. Just remember that offering care is not enough. Your practice must offer the best care available. That includes being sensitive to the patient as a consumer with needs and rights. As an employee, one wants to look forward to working in a safe environment. However, the health care field does have perils and pitfalls. By being informed, using common sense, and following the rules, one can avoid these pitfalls and retain your doctor (along with your job). That way everyone benefits!

APPENDIX
FORMS

Release of Medical Information

I, ____ hereby request my
medical information including the diagnosis and records of any treatment or examination
rendered to me to be released to the below mentioned person/persons:

____

____

____

____

____
Signature

____
Witness

Form 1. Records Release.

Eyesight Associates

PATIENT INFORMATION SHEET

Date_______________

Welcome to our office. Please complete all forms, front and back. Return to the receptionist, who will use the information to prepare your chart. Thank you.

_________________ _________________ _________________ _________________
First Name   Middle Name   Preferred Name   Last Name

Address_________________________________ City, State & Zip _________________________________

Home Phone _________________________   Male/Female   Single / Married / Widowed / Separated / Divorced

Social Security # _________________________ Date of Birth _________________________ Age ______

Employer _________________________ Work Address _________________________ Work Phone _________________

Are you retired? Yes / No   Date Retired _________________

Who referred you to our office? ____

Whom to notify in case of an emergency? _________________________________ Relationship _______________

Address _________________________ Work Phone _________________ Home Phone _________________

SPOUSE INFORMATION

Spouse Name _________________________________ Spouse Work Phone _________________________

Retired? Yes / No   Date Retired _________________

Employed By _________________________________ Occupation _________________________________

Business Address ____

PLEASE COMPLETE IF PATIENT IS UNDER 18

Name of Father _________________________________ Employer _________________________________

Employer Address / Phone ____

Name of Mother _________________________________ Employer _________________________________

Employer Address / Phone ____

INSURANCE INFORMATION

Primary Insurance _________________________________ Address _________________________________

Policy # _________________________ Group # _________________ Policy Holder Name _________________________

Is this an HMO? Yes / No   Do you need a referral / precert to be seen? Yes / No

Secondary Insurance _________________________________ Address _________________________________

Policy # _________________________ Group # _________________ Policy Holder Name _________________________

Is this an HMO? Yes / No   Do you need a referral / precert to be seen? Yes / No

Vision Plan Name _________________________ Policy # _________________________ Group # _________________

Form 2. Initial Patient Registration (continued).

RESPONSIBLE PARTY

All charges are due at the time of service unless we are participating with your insurance company, then we will file and expect payment within 45 days. You are responsible for any unmet deductibles, copayment or noncovered services.

Are you personally responsible for the payment of yours fees? Yes / No

If yes, will you be paying by: Cash / Check / Visa / Master Card / Discover

If no, who will be responsible? Name____ DOB ____________

Relationship to you _________________Address _______________________________ Phone ______________

AUTHORIZATIONS

Authorization for treatment

I hereby authorize and request medical treatment by the Eyesight Associates staff. I further authorize the performance of whatever procedure the judgment of the above-named staff may deem necessary during any treatment. I also authorize the administration of any anesthetics and analgesics which above staff may deem advisable. (Note: Eye drops and eye medications are considered anesthetics and analgesics.)

Financial Agreement

I acknowledge that payment is due at the time of treatment, unless other arrangements have been made. I accept full financial responsibility for all charges not covered by my insurance company. The above information is accurate and complete to the best of my knowledge.

Assignment of Benefits

All insurance forms processed by this office require assignment of benefits to this practice unless payment in full is made. Your cooperation in complying with the terms of this assignment is appreciated. I, the undersigned, hereby authorize payment of medical and surgical benefits directly to EYESIGHT ASSOCIATES.

Authorization to Release Information

I hereby authorize my doctor / doctors to furnish the insurance company all information necessary to secure payment of benefits.

____   ____
Patient / Parent or Guardian Signature   Date

Form 2. Initial Patient Registration (continued).

Eyesight Associates

Name ____ Date of Birth _________________ Date___________

Name of Referring Physician _________________________________ Location _____________________________________

REVIEW OF SYSTEMS

Do you currently or have you ever had a problem with any of the following: *(please check)*

YES   NO

☐   ☐   Ear, Nose, Mouth, Throat ____

☐   ☐   Cardiovascular (Heart / High Blood Pressure) ____

☐   ☐   Respiratory (Lung / Breathing) ____

☐   ☐   Gastrointestinal (Stomach / Intestines) ____

☐   ☐   Genitourinary (Genital / Kidneys / Bladder)____

☐   ☐   Musculoskeletal (Muscle / Arthritis / Joints) ____

☐   ☐   Integumentary (Skin) ____

☐   ☐   Neurological / Psychiatric (Depression / Nerves) ____

☐   ☐   Endocrine (Diabetes / Thyroid / etc.) ____

☐   ☐   Hematologic (Anemia / Bleeding Tendencies) ____

☐   ☐   Lymphatic (Swelling) ____

☐   ☐   Allergic / Immunologic ____

Do you have any allergies to any medications (Please list) ____

Currently taking any medications (Please list) ____

List any surgeries you have had. ____
____

FAMILY AND SOCIAL HISTORY:

Do any of <u>your family</u> members have any of the following diseases:

☐   ☐   Glaucoma ____

☐   ☐   Cataracts ____

☐   ☐   Retinal / Macular Degeneration ____

☐   ☐   Arthritis ____

☐   ☐   Cancer ____

☐   ☐   Diabetes ____

☐   ☐   Heart Attack ____

☐   ☐   High Blood Pressure ____

☐   ☐   Kidney Disease ____

☐   ☐   Stroke ____

☐   ☐   Other ____

Current Occupation: ____

Do you smoke?   Yes   No   How many packs per day? _______________________________________

Do you drink alcohol?   Yes   No   How often?

Additional Information:

____
____
____
____
____

Form 2. Initial Patient Registration (continued).

PATIENT INFORMATION UPDATE

Welcome, we are delighted to see you again!

Please take a few minutes to help us update our records.

Name ____ Today's Date ______________
     FIRST   MIDDLE   LAST

1. Has your name changed since your last visit here? ________ Yes ________ No

   If yes, what was the old name? ____

   What name do you use for health insurance if different than above? ______________________

   ____

2. If you have a new or different address since your initial visit here, please indicate below:

   ____

   ____

   ____

3. Has your marital status changed? ________ Yes ________ No

4. Has your telephone number changed? ________ Yes ________ No

   Please indicate your correct telephone number ____

5. Has your employment changed? ________ Yes ________ No

   Please indicate your new employer name and address:

   ____

   ____

   ____

       New employer telephone #: ________________________________

6. Have you changed health insurance companies? ________ Yes ________ No

   If yes, please indicate your new health insurance carrier and address.

   Primary ____________________________________   Secondary ____________________________________

   ____________________________________   ____________________________________

   ____________________________________   ____________________________________

   Group Nos. ________________________________   Group Nos. ________________________________

   Subscriber Nos. ____________________________   Subscriber Nos. ____________________________

7. Who is responsible for this bill? ____

8. Please note any changes in your health since your last visit.

       Illness ____

       Accident ____

       Allergies ____

       Medications being taken ____

       ____

       Other ____

       ____

       ____

9. Signature ____

Form 3. Interval Visit Registration.

Supplier's Notice:

Medicare will only pay for services that it determines to be "reasonable and necessary" under Section 1862(a)(1) of the Medicare law. If Medicare determines that a particular service, although it would otherwise by covered, is not "reasonable and necessary" under Medicare program standards, Medicare will deny payment for that service. I believe that, in your case, Medicare is likely to deny payment for

____ (specify the particular service), for the following reasons ____

_________________________________ (give reason[s] for your belief).

Beneficiary's Acknowledgment and Agreement to Pay:

I have been notified by my supplier that he or she believes that, in my case, Medicare is likely to deny payment for the services identified above, for the reason stated. If Medicare denies the payment, I agree to be personally and fully responsible for payment.

Date __________

Signed____
(beneficiary signature)

Form 4. Authorization for Payment.

Medicare Limitation of Liability

Medicare will only pay for services that it determines to be "reasonable and necessary." If Medicare determines that a particular service, although it would otherwise be covered, is "not reasonable and necessary" under Medicare program standards, Medicare will deny payment for that service. I believe that, in your case, Medicare is likely to deny payment for one or more of the following reasons:

____ Medicare usually does not pay for this service.

____ Medicare does not pay for this because it is a treatment that has not been proved effective.

____ Medicare usually does not pay for like services by more than one doctor during the same time period.

____ Medicare usually does not pay for like services by more than one doctor of the same specialty.

____ Medicare usually does not pay for such an extensive procedure.

____ Medicare usually does not pay for the supply of the equipment/medication.

Should either of these determinations be made by Medicare B, you agree that you have been informed and that you agree to be responsible for payment of the services listed below.

Procedure   Charge

Patient Signature______________________________

Date______________

Form 5. Authorization for Responsibility.

Noncovered Services and Materials Form—Medicare

I understand that I am personally responsible for the following services and/or materials that are not covered by Medicare and/other insurance.

Refraction

____

____

____

Deluxe Frame Purchase—Medicare

Having been informed that an extra charge is being made by the physician or supplier for deluxe frames, this extra charge is not covered by Medicare and that standard frames are available at no extra charge, I have chosen to purchase deluxe frames from the suppliers.

Deluxe frame coverage

____

____

____

____

Date _______________________   Total ____

Name ____

Form 6. Waiver of Liability.

Disclosure and Consent
Eye Procedures

Medical and Surgical Procedures

To the patient: You have the right, as a patient, to be informed about your condition and the recommended surgical, medical, or diagnostic procedure to be used so that you may make the decision whether or not to undergo the procedure after knowing the risks and hazards involved. This disclosure is not meant to scare or alarm you; it is simply an effort to make you better informed so you may give or withhold your consent to the procedure.

I (we), ____, voluntarily
(patient's name)
request Dr. ___________________________________as my (our) physician, and such associates, technical assistants, and other health care providers as they may deem necessary, to treat my condition that has been explained to me (us) as:

____

____

____

____

I (we) understand that the following surgical, medical, and/or diagnostic procedures are planned for me, and I (we) voluntarily consent to and authorize these procedures:

____

____

____

____

I (we) understand that I (we) may revoke this consent at any time before such procedures are performed, and that such revocation will not influence or prejudice my (our) ability to obtain alternate care.

Form 7. Informed Consent (continued).

I (we) understand that my (our) physician may discover other or different conditions that require additional or different procedures than those planned. I (we) authorize my (our) physician, and such associates, technical assistants, and other health care providers to perform such other procedures that are advisable in their professional judgment.

I (we) (do) (do not) consent to the use of blood and blood products as deemed necessary.

I (we) (do) (do not) consent to the taking of photographs of me by my (our) physician, and such associates, technical assistants, and other health care providers before, during, and/or after the performance of the surgical, medical, and/or diagnostic procedures planned for me and to the use and custody of such photographs and negatives thereof for educational purposes by my (our) physician.

I (we) understand that no warranty or guarantee has been made to me (us) as to a result or cure.

Just as there may be risks and hazards in continuing my present condition without treatment, there are also risks and hazards related to the performance of the surgical, medical, and/or diagnostic procedures planned for me. I (we) realize that common to surgical, medical, and/or diagnostic procedures is the potential for infection, blood clots in veins and lungs, hemorrhage, allergic reactions, and even death. I (we) also realize that other risks and hazards, not listed above, may occur in connection with this particular procedure as explained by my (our) physician:

____

____

Form 7. Informed Consent (continued).

Eye Treatments and Procedures

A. Advancement or recession of eye muscles (correction of strabismus).
    i. Decrease in vision.
    ii. Double vision.
B. Extraction of lens for cataract with or without implantation of intraocular lens.
    i. Partial or total loss of vision.
    ii. Complications requiring additional treatment.
    iii. Need for glasses or contact lenses.
    iv. Complications requiring the removal of implanted lens.
    v. Ptosis (droopy eyelid).
C. Retinal detachment surgery.
    i. Recurrence of detachment.
    ii. Partial or total loss of vision.
    iii. Complications requiring additional treatment.
    iv. Ptosis (droopy eyelid).

I (we) understand that anesthesia involves additional risks and hazards, but I (we) request the use of anesthetics for the relief and protection from pain during the planned and additional procedures. I (we) realize the anesthesia may have to be changed possibly without explanation to me (us).

I (we) understand that certain complications may result from the use of any anesthetic including respiratory problems, drug reaction, paralysis, brain damage, or even death. Other risks and hazards that may result from the use of general anesthetics range from minor discomfort to injury to vocal cords, teeth, or eyes. I (we) understand that other risks and hazards resulting from spinal or epidural anesthetics include headache and chronic pain.

I (we) have been given an opportunity to ask questions about my conditions, alternative forms of anesthesia and treatment, risks of nontreatment, the procedures to be used, and the risks and hazards involved, and I (we) believe that I (we) have sufficient information to give this informed consent.

Form 7. Informed Consent (continued).

I (we) certify that this form of Disclosure and Consent has been fully explained to me (us), that I (we) have read it or have had it read to me (us), that the blank spaces have been filled in, and that I (we) understand its contents.

Date _________________________   Time:___________________ ___AM ___PM

____
Signature of patient/other legally responsible person

Witness:

____
Name

____
Address (street or PO box)

____
City, state, zip code

Form 7. Informed Consent (continued).

Applicant ____

Date ____

Name of Interviewer ____

Questions   Comments

1. Why would you like to work with us?

2. Where did you learn the skills mentioned in our ad?

3. Why did you leave your last job?

4. Do you like working with other employees?

5. Do you like meeting people for the first time?

6. We get a bit pushed here sometimes.
   How would you feel about that?

7. Are you interested in learning other skills?

8. How do you feel about pressing people to
   pay for eyewear?

9. Do you think it's best to stay home with a cold?

10. Are you willing to be bonded?

Form 8. Interview Response Chart.

Name _______________________________________ Date_______________

Job title ____ Current salary _______

Starting date of employment _________________________________

Date of last review ____

Cooperation

Does this employee show the ability and willingness to get along with coworkers?
Points

5	An exceptional team worker. Flexible.
4	Is usually agreeable, tactful, and obliging.
3	Goes along willingly.
2	Is sometimes uncooperative.
1	Tends to cause friction.

Dependability

How reliable is the employee in meeting his or her work schedule?
Points

5	Places office interests ahead of personal conveniences.
4	Is punctual. Does not waste time.
3	Is generally on the job as needed.
2	Some abuses. Occasionally needs to be admonished.
1	Chronic abuses of work schedule.

Initiative

How well does this employee begin an assignment direction and recognize the best way of doing it?
Points

5	Self-starter. Makes practical suggestions.
4	Proceeds on assigned work voluntarily and readily accepts suggestions.
3	Does regular work without prompting.
2	Relies on others. Needs help getting started.
1	Must usually be told exactly what to do.

Form 9. Employee Appraisal (continued).

Job Knowledge

How well does this employee understand the job to which he/she has been assigned?
Points

5	Thoroughly understands all aspects.
4	Has more than adequate knowledge of the job.
3	Has sufficient knowledge of some phases.
2	Has insufficient knowledge of some phases.
1	Continually needs instructions.

Leadership

Is the employee capable of supervising others?
Points

5	An exceptional leader and organizer.
4	Plans work well. Poised, respected.
3	Has adequate leadership qualities.
2	Potential leader but needs development.
1	Poor planner and organizer. Fails to develop and inspire others.

Awareness

Is the employee genuinely concerned how the patient/consumer is made welcome to the office/dispensary?
Points

5	Always shows concern about the patient/consumer's welfare and comfort.
4	Is usually careful about the patient/consumer's feelings.
3	Has average concern for the patient/consumer's feelings.
2	Is sometimes rude and inconsiderate of the patient/consumer.
1	Never regards interest of the patient/consumer. Patient/consumers have complained about employee.

Personal Work Habits

How accurate, neat, and complete are the employee's work habits?
Points

5	Is always neat, accurate, and thorough.
4	Makes few mistakes. Careful worker.
3	Work is acceptable.
2	Is occasionally careless. Needs checking.
1	Is inaccurate and careless.

Form 9. Employee Appraisal (continued).

Responsibility

How does this employee accept all the responsibilities of the job?

Points

5	Accepts all responsibilities fully and meets emergencies.
4	Conscientiously tries to fulfill job responsibilities.
3	Accepts but does not seek responsibility.
2	Does some assigned tasks reluctantly.
1	Is indifferent. Avoids responsibilities.

Desire to Improve Quality of Optical Care to Patients/Consumers

Does the employee contribute to the improvement of optical eyecare to patients/consumers?

Points

5	Is mostly warm, outgoing, and smiles.
4	Is somewhat warm, outgoing, and smiles.
3	Is inconsistent.
2	Rarely is warm, outgoing, or smiles.
1	Is cool and detached.

Ability to Affect Office Productivity

How does the employee try to affect office productivity?

Points

5	Frequently suggests cost savings and promotes office.
4	Occasionally suggests cost savings and promotes office.
3	Rarely suggests cost savings and promotes office.
2	Is apathetic.
1	Is wasteful and negative.

Exhibits Enthusiasm for One's Work

Employee exhibits enthusiasm for work by:

Points

5	Being most positive and happy.
4	Being somewhat positive and happy.
3	Is occasionally positive and happy.
2	Is rarely positive and happy.
1	Is never positive and happy.

Form 9. Employee Appraisal (continued).

Willingness to Accept New Assignments

Does the employee present a willingness to accept a new assignment?
Points

5	Seeks out new assignments.
4	Gladly accepts the challenge of new assignments.
3	Accepts new assignments.
2	Rarely accepts new assignments.
1	Avoids new assignments.

Attendance

Does the employee report to work:

Points

5	Rarely misses (less than 6 sick days per year).
4	Misses average amount (4 sick days per year).
3	Misses allowed amount (6 sick days per year).
2	Misses more than allowed amount.
1	Misses frequently.

Punctuality

How does the employee prepare for the work day?
Points

5	Always prepares ahead of time.
4	Sometimes prepares ahead of time.
3	Prepares on time.
2	Sometimes prepares late.
1	Frequently prepares late.

Loyalty (Seniority)

How does the employee exhibit loyalty to the employer?
Points

5	Employee worked for more than 5 years.
4	Employee worked for more than 4 years.
3	Employee worked for more than 3 years.
2	Employee worked for more than 2 years.
1	Employee worked for more than 1 year.

Form 9. Employee Appraisal (continued).

Development of New Skills

Has the employee demonstrated the development of new skills?

Points

5	Has developed more than one new skill.
4	Has developed one new skill.
3	Has worked on developing new skills.
2	Has expressed interest, but not worked on developing new skills.
1	Has never developed new skills.

Point Evaluation

16 Categories X 5 possible points = 80 possible points

Rating Score

72–80	Excellent
64–71	Good
56–63	Average
48–55	Below average

(Use space below for added comments.)

____

____

____

____

____

____

____

____

____

____

____

____

Date discussed with employee_______________________________

Employee's signature ____

Form 9. Employee Appraisal (continued).

FROM:

Name ___________________________ Date ___________________

Department ___________________________ Position ___________________

____

RE:

Employee ___________________________ Position ___________________

1. I have made the following observation of an employee's conduct:

2. I have informed the employee of the following standards that will be expected from him/her in the future.

3. These standards are important because of the following impact on the work environment.

4. I have advised the employee of the following consequences if he/she fails to follow the above standards:

Form 10. Employee Warning (continued).

5. These matters will be reviewed within _______________ days.

____

Supervisor

I have read and received a copy of the above statement. I do/do not wish to submit written comments of my own about this matter.

____

Employee

Form 10. Employee Warning (continued).

Name of Employee ____

Date of incident ____

Witnesses to the incident ____

____

Description of incident ____

____

____

____

____

____

____

____

____

Action taken to prevent further incidents of this kind ____

____

____

____

____

____

____

____

____

____

Signature of Employee   Date

Signature of Employee's Supervisor   Date

President   Date

Form 11. Incident Report.

October 22, 1996

Bill Borover
555 Drive Lane
City, State 00055

Dear Hiring Manager:

Enclosed please find my résumé in response to your August 13th ad in the Anytown Times/Ledger for a position as a clinical assistant. Of particular interest were your requirements in the areas of staff development, diagnostics, and skill building for less-experienced staff. Outlined below are my accomplishments that support the qualification expectations.

My background includes four years of experience in optometric assisting and optical sales for Gracie Eye Center. During this period, I compiled an excellent track record in training and production. This effectiveness is reflected by:

1. Increasing the number of patients seen in the clinic daily.
2. Promoting eyewear sales.
3. Training more people to do visual fields.

During my four-year history with Gracie Ophthalmology, I never lost track of a patient or received a disagreeable note. For this reason, I believe my credentials are especially appealing. I am confident that your practice will benefit from having me as part of your organization.

I am strongly interested in the position and would welcome the opportunity for a direct discussion of your needs. You can reach me at 1-619-555-8055 after 6 AM.

Your consideration of my unique qualifications is greatly appreciated.

Sincerely,

Bill Borover

Form 12. Sample Cover Letter.

TAMMY BELLAMY, COT
203 Sheffield Drive
Danville, PA 12345
Phone and Fax 1-112-555-1193

SUMMARY:	Six years in ophthalmic assisting, Certified Ophthalmic Technician, Assisting in Low Vision certification, surgical counseling and assisting. Especially good with senior adults.
OBJECTIVE:	To obtain a position as an ophthalmic technician.
EXPERIENCE: 1994 to present	OPHTHALMIC TECHNICIAN James Lambda, MD. Center for Eye Care, 123 Main Street, Chula Vista, CA 12345. Phone 1-706-555-9876. Basic patient work-ups including history and exam, retinoscopy, refractometry, tonometry, A-scan, potential acuity meter, glare test. Assisting in surgery. Staff training. Dictate and transcribe physician's correspondence. Established no-show follow-up program. Other duties included formal Goldmann perimetry, minor surgery assisting, medical supply ordering.
1990 to 1994	OPHTHALMIC TECHNICIAN AND LOW VISION SPECIALIST Willard Langley, MD. 564 Center Street, Macon, GA 68574. Phone 1-912-555-4937. Basic patient work-ups including history and exam, refractometry, A-scan, fundus photography. Automated (Humphrey) and Goldmann fields. Surgical counselor from 1990 to 1992. In 1992 helped establish practice's low vision clinic and was assigned as manager. Other assorted duties included automated perimetry, Tangent screen, minor surgery assisting, fundus photography, staff training.
CERTIFICATION:	Assisting in Low Vision certification, 1993 Certified Ophthalmic Technician, 1992 Certified Ophthalmic Assistant, 1991
EDUCATION:	AS, Columbus College, 1989 Major: General Studies (Biology emphasis)
ACTIVITIES:	Member of Association of Technical Personnel in Ophthalmology.
OTHER SKILLS:	Word processing. Subject searching with National Library of Medicine via MedLine.

Form 13. Sample Résumé.

Index